CLIMBERS GUIDE TO MONTANA

The scenes we gaze upon from our autos are getting old. There is a long, long trail a-winding into the land of our dreams and the Montana Mountaineers dream of it first and then go and see it for themselves.

Glenn Boyer, Secretary
Montana Mountaineers
1922

CLIMBERS GUIDE
TO MONTANA

Pat Caffrey

Mountain Press Publishing Company

Missoula

Copyright © 1986
Mountain Press Publishing Co.

Library of Congress Cataloging-in-Publication Data

Caffrey, Pat.
 The climbers guide to Montana.

 Rock climbing—Montana—Guide-books. 2. Montana—
Description and travel —1981-   —Guide-books. I Title.

GV199.42.M9C34 1986   917.86   86-8426
ISBN 0-87842-201-3 (pbk.)

Acknowledgments

I wish to thank the following individuals for their valuable assistance in the creation of this book. Some of these folks provided generously of their specific knowledge of individual peaks, routes, and rock climbing areas. Others offered general ideas concerning content and climbing ethics. One or two suggested I scrap the entire project. All are true mountaineers in the Montana spirit. I enjoyed talking with them, and I hope this finished product accounts for their concerns as well as reflects their enthusiasm: Ed Anacker, Bob Anderson, Tom Ballard, Donny Black, Warren Bowman, Sam Braxton, Ray Breuninger, Pat Callas, Chad Chadwick, Tom Cladouhos, Gary Cook, Bill Cunningham, Chuck Dalby, Al Day, Rex Dougherty, Elliott Dubreuil, J. Gordon Edwards, Harrison Fagg, John Gogas, Rick Graetz, Dexter Hale, George Howe, Neil Hulbert, Paul Jensen, Terry Kennedy, Jerry Kogan, Dave Line, Mavis Lorenz, Ed Madej, Mike McCann, Bill Morgan, Bill Myers, Todd Onken, Bill Pursell, Alvin Randall, Rick Reese, Greg Rice, Mike Sample, Carl Sanders, Don Scharfe, Jack Tackle, Graham Thompson, Jim Ullrich, Bill Weiland, Dave Wessel, John Westenberg, Dave Whitesitt, and Keith Yale.

I also obtained help from many government offices, including the Forest Service Region I Headquarters (Bill Worf and Jim Dolan); Beaverhead National Forest (Arnie Royce); Bitterroot National Forest (Chuck Troxel); Bridger Wilderness, Wyoming, concerning climber impact on wilderness areas (Dave Hohl); Custer National Forest (John Gibson); Red Lodge Ranger District (Tom Alt), Fort Howes Ranger District (Rod Schaeffer); Deerlodge National Forest; Flathead National Forest (Mike Conner, Cal Tassinari); Gallatin National Forest (Ross McPherson, Terry Johnson, Joe Gutkoski); Helena National Forest (Wayne Worthington); Lewis and Clark National Forest (Ed Kinsman, Wayne Phillips); Lolo National Forest (Homer Boyce, Milo McLeod); Kootenai National Forest (Lance Schelvan); Bureau of Land Management—Butte Office; Confederated Salish and Kootenai Tribe (Dave Rockwell, Herschel May); and Glacier National Park (Rich Altemus, Oak Blair, Bill Conrod, Gerry DeSanto, Bob Frauson, Dick Mattson, Dave Panebaker, and Joe Reis).

Fire lookout status was updated using the 1984 edition of Ray Kresek's *Fire Lookouts of the Northwest*, a most extraordinary book, available from W. 123 Westview, Spokane, WA 99218.

Dave Alt of the University of Montana Geology Department was kind enough to give me a crash course in Montana geology.

Minuteman Aviation (Missoula), Strand Aviation (Kalispell), and Yellowstone Air Service (Livingston) were very helpful in setting me in the proper position for the aerial photos used in this book.

The following people and organizations graciously provided many of the photographs found in this book: Bureau of Land Management (Dean Littlepage—Butte), Bill Cunningham, Ann Felstead, Raymond Gehman, *Kalispell Weekly News*, Marvin McDonald's family, Roger Marshall, Rick Reese, Randy Sandin, Cal Tassinari, Jim Ullrich, U.S. Forest Service (Bob Neaves, Don Comstock, Joyce Hailey—Missoula; Becky Timmons—Old Lookouts Project), and Lefty Young. Jon Schulman Photography of Missoula did the painstaking work of converting color slides to black and white prints, and Jennifer Stackpole and Bryan Steubs of Flying Zebra Photo Lab did the very large job of photo-finishing negatives.

Mary Marshall typed the final draft.

Dedication

Most climbing accidents are caused by carelessness and ignorance. Yet it must be said that some injuries and fatalities will happen regardless of how careful climbers are. If the mountains were perfectly predictable, there would be no lure to go or freedom once we got there. Danger is an inevitable part of climbing.

Marvin McDonald was an accomplished and careful Montana mountaineer who perished in the Tetons in July of 1981. He had the support and appreciation of his family, although they were aware of the dangers involved. On the preceding page is a picture of him in the Bitterroots, and below is the McDonald family at a ceremony where a tree was planted on the University of Montana campus in Marvin's memory. These photos are a warning to remember your family, but they are also a statement that a full awareness of life lies somewhere near the edge of death.

Raymond Gehman

"I do not regret this journey; we took risks, we knew we took them, things have come out against us, therefore we have no cause for complaint."
—Captain Scott's Last Journal

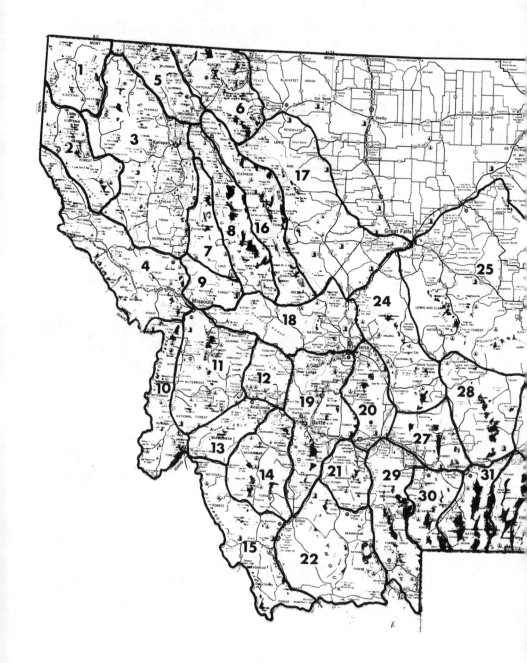

Range Map of Montana

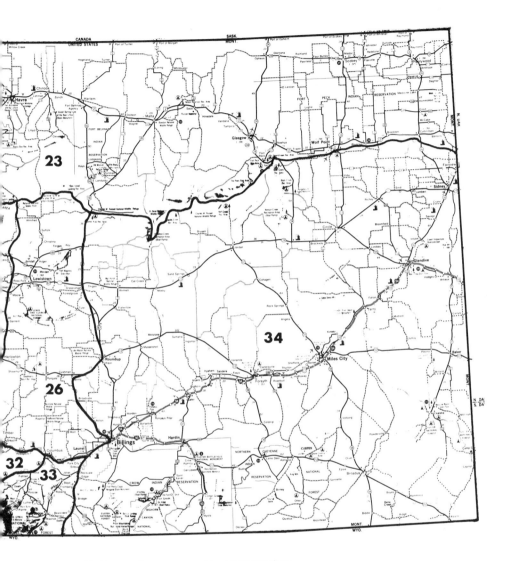

NOTE: Map numbers correspond to chapter numbers.

Table of Contents

Acknowledgments 5
Dedication...6
Range Map of Montana 8
Foreword..11
How to Use This Book 12
Climbing in Montana 15
Warning to Mountaineers..24
I Told You So 25
Wildland Management: An Essay for Climbers 30

   1.   Purcell Mountains 35
   2.   Cabinet Mountains 39
   3.   Salish Mountains..43
   4.   Coeur d'Alene Mountains 47
   5.   Whitefish Range..53
   6.   Glacier National Park 57
   7.   Mission Range..71
   8.   Swan Range 79
   9.   Rattlesnake Mountains...89
 10.   Bitterroot Mountains 93
 11.   Sapphire Mountains 103
 12.   Flint Creek Range 107
 13.   Anaconda Range 109
 14.   Pioneer Mountains 113
 15.   Beaverhead Mountains 119
 16.   Flathead Range 123
 17.   Rocky Mountain Front 129
 18.   Garnet Range Area 135
 19.   Boulder Batholith Area 139
 20.   Elkhorn Mountains 145
 21.   Tobacco Root Mountains 149
 22.   Ruby River Ranges...153
 23.   North Prairie 159
 24.   Big Belt Mountains...165
 25.   Little Belt Mountains...169
 26.   Snowy Mountains...173
 27.   Bridger Range 177
 28.   Crazy Mountains...179
 29.   Madison Range 185
 30.   Gallatin Range..191
 31.   Absaroka Range—West 195
 32.   Absaroka Range—East 201
 33.   Beartooth Range 205
 34.   Lower Yellowstone Area..213

Horizons..219
Glossary..235

Foreword

"In hopes of finding a friend in you
I'll take you to see a magnificent view.
On the edges of canyons so deep in the earth
I'll show you a path to personal worth."

—Richard Ladzinski

(found in the summit register of Mt. Cowan)

There's beauty out there, and it's not always untouched by the hand of man. It's your own footprints in the snow of a summit ridge, a register box glimpsed over the last outcrop, farmlands and cities far below, your beat-up old car back at the trailhead. You can defer getting upset about some road, clear-cut, mine, or microwave site. It won't make the trees look artificial. The peaks won't lose their shine. Mountains provide an opportunity to re-evaluate preconceptions and transcend predictable irritations. From his high place a mountaineer brings his insights and love back down to give others, for he has realized there is something invulnerable in him.

One summer night I spread my bedroll on the sage flats on the east side of the Tobacco Root Mountains. At two a.m. the moon was shining brightly and I was fast asleep. Suddenly I was awakened by a deafening roar and a blinding flash of light. A B-52 jet bomber on a radar evasion practice run, 400' above the ground, was passing directly overhead. I watched its landing lights run across the rocks and trees. Was my wilderness experience shattered?

We humans control so very little on this planet. Even the forces we've harnessed are greater than we are. So many of us are out to "preserve the environment" but very few of us can even properly perceive it. As that bomber roared up those slopes I was soon to climb, practicing its ability to defend our country or destroy the world (I didn't know which), I was thrilled, and glad to be a climber—seeking the high places for no other reason than to perceive the environment.

May this book show you the way to new heights of perception.

Pat Caffrey
Seeley Lake
1985

How to Use This Book

Montana's mountains are a paradox. Elsewhere one can find higher peaks, cleaner rock, and well-defined routes. But here the peaks lie on the horizon in lingering obscurity. One finds vast solitude, unobtrusive challenge, and more sheer diversity than probably any other place of comparable size. Montana is representative of all the geologic processes that formed the continent, and is the meeting ground of many climates as well. There are 34 range groups in this book, and each is unique. Within these groups are sub-ranges which also exhibit extensive variety. Each is a different world of climbing, and this is a different kind of climbing guide.

Basic Premises: This book doesn't attempt to "hype" certain areas or downplay others, but simply tries to do justice to what's out there, and follows the lead of public land managers by advocating dispersed use in hopes of minimizing regulations. Except where such information is critical or appropriate, the book will not attempt to lead you by the hand from vehicle to summit. Nor will it describe every little fantastic revelation you are likely to discover, every pretty thing, every wrong turn, every particular hazard. Much of the pleasure of climbing Montana's mountains is in discovering your own route, feeling the excitement and spirit of a pioneer in high places which Montana climbers still enjoy. This book will suggest ways you can attack the mountain of your choice without extensive reconnaissance, and will tell you if your level of climbing competence and skill are adequate. It should also whet your appetite, then take you to a point where the unknown and unspeakable begins.

Mountain Descriptions: All prominent peaks are listed. Since nearly all of them can be ascended non-technically by several approaches, the suggested route is, generally speaking, the easiest. Other appealing routes are sometimes pointed out. Technical routes are also sometimes mentioned for the climber who isn't satisfied with the easiest route but seeks out some way that really *is* impossible. Technical opportunities on the various spires and walls are mentioned separately at the end of each chapter. You won't find dotted-line diagrams, or elaborate descriptions and decimal ratings for all the moves. You won't find out who made the first ascent, did the most difficult variant, did it without protection, etc. You will find general ratings, and enough information to provide a working knowledge of all the places you can jam, lay back, and rappell.

This book is not a substitute for the ability to find and evaluate your route, change your plans according to time and conditions or know where you are.

For each range the peaks are listed from west to east within groups, starting with the northernmost group and working south. Where possible, specific sub-ranges or areas are identified. The common, accepted name of the peak is listed. Unnamed peaks are listed as elevation points. If the peak has a local or assumed name, then the elevation of that point is listed as its name, followed by the unaccepted or unmapped name in parentheses. All peaks with map names are followed by their elevation. If various maps give different elevations, then the higher one is listed, unless the most recent topographic map specifies the lower elevation. Following the elevation is the rating code, consisting of a capital letter in brackets. It indicates the level of skill required to ascend the peak by the easiest route, and only the easiest route. The rating is *not* a measure of exasperation. It does not imply how much time the climb will take, or make any assumption as to your level of physical or mental conditioning.

Ascending an S-rated route. Note that the hands are used only for balance and resting.

On a C-rated climb, your arms hold you in a position for your next move. —Kalispell Weekly News

D—Drive: You can reach the summit in your automobile. Brakes should be in good working condition. Ideal for persons who otherwise would never get to a mountaintop for various reasons. A great family trip.

P—Primitive Road: OK for two-wheel drive pickups and some autos with high ground clearance, under good conditions. The road conditions may vary with the weather, and occasionally that means the road is not suited for cars under any conditions. Four-wheel drive may prove useful in some instances.

J—Jeep Trail: Seldom passable to two-wheel drive vehicles. These routes sometimes deteriorate to the point where even four-wheel drive vehicles have problems and it becomes easier to walk.

W—Walk or Hike: The route is usually a trail. It is either marked or obvious, and route-finding ability isn't necessary. Brief strolls through high meadows and other easy ground where the route is simple, short, and straightforward fall into this classification.

S—Scramble: Cross-country travel where route-finding ability is required. Varies from easy rolling terrain to timber and brush to extensive loose rock and boulder fields. It's distinguished from more difficult ratings in that your legs will do all the work. On more difficult scrambles, you may choose short pitches of C-rated terrain in the interests of route efficiency.

C—Climb: More specifically, a hand climb. High-angle rock. The hands and arms are used to pull or support you on the route, not just for balance or during a slip. A moderate degree of exposure is often involved. Beginners may wish tc rope up and be belayed for security. In winter or when wet, these routes become technical and may require rappelling. They are not suited for your dog.

T—Technical: Protection is required and exposure is explicit. Glacier traverses requiring ropes also fall in this category. Direct aid is not necessary on any T-rated peak listed if climbed by the suggested easiest route, but may be employed on more difficult routes as well as on spires and walls. Downclimbing a T-rated mountain usually involves some rappelling.

This classification system is general in order to be suitable for the many different kinds of rock found in the various ranges. For the benefit of those used to using other classifications, the following conversions provide rough equivalents:

Glacier National Park Classification:
Class 1   equal to W or very easy S
Class 2 & 3   equal to S
Class 4   equal to C
Class 5 & 6   equal to T

American Alpine System (Decimal):
Class 2 equal to W
Class 3 equal to S
Class 4 equal to C
Class 5 equal to T—Protected free climbing: 5.1 (easy) to 5.13 (extreme difficulty)
Class 6 equal to T—Direct aid

Following the peak name, elevation, and rating is a description of the suggested approach. "Register" indicates that a register was placed on the summit and can be found unless something has since happened to it. The directions given *always* use the summit as the central compass point. "Trail to southwest" means there is a trail southwest of the peak. "Northeast ridge" identifies a ridge that radiates out northeast from the summit.

■ Selected peaks have directions in detail with a photo and map. These peaks are prominent, have straightforward routes, and serve as an introduction to the kind of mountain experience to be found on other peaks in the same range.

Kalispell Weekly News

Climbing in Montana

"The trick is to suit the style to the climb and to oneself. The truly ultimate style is the perfect match—the treading of that fine edge between ambition and ability."
—Royal Robbins

Indians used to climb hills and mountains in Montana to scout buffalo herds or conduct vision quests. On a quest, an Indian would climb alone to a summit, often fasting and taking risks, with strength of will and a desire to walk in the ways of the Great Spirit.

With the coming of the white man, unrecorded scrambles doubtlessly were made by trappers, prospectors, army scouts, and generally lost individuals. After the beginning of this century, surveyors explored the ranges establishing control points on prominent peaks, and their remote hardships and exploits will never be repeated. The first recorded major ascent occurred in 1892 when Henry Stimson (later to become Secretary of War during World War II) and two friends pioneered a classic route up the east face of Chief Mountain on the edge of what is now Glacier National Park. Twenty years later, fire lookouts began to crop up in the solitude of the forested ranges, finally occupying a total of 626 high points. In time, all the state's major peaks were climbed, though it was not until the 1970s that the last of the 12000' peaks in the Beartooths was ascended. Technical rock climbing did not really get going until the 1960s, and there are some remote granitic areas which have yet to be tested.

With increased wildland use in the early 1970s, individuals deliberately downplayed certain areas. Perhaps they did so to preserve the frustrations they faced so that the rewards they had realized would still be available. At present, informal climbing workshops are sometimes set up by local groups, but genuine climbing schools and guide services have not been established, even in Glacier National Park. There seems to be little demand for them.

Those who don't care to deal with the unexpected won't enjoy climbing in Montana. Roads become closed, gated, washed out. One can bushwhack through heavy brush and timber, only to find an unmapped road near timberline. New roads and logging obliterate or change the location of trailheads. The trails themselves become overgrown or relocated, and their signs and markers fall down and decay. Maps sometimes show trails that were never built, and some apparently going straight up cliffs or over mislocated peaks. Existing maintained trails may be temporarily blocked for miles by fresh blowdown or mud, and their length may be double what you measure on a map due to curves and detours. Once off the trail, you may find ground which looks easy on a topographic map turning out to be broken up or covered with brush and downfall. Finally, the mountains themselves are dynamic and constantly changing. A several-

"I'm sorry. The number you have reached is not in service at this time." Lookouts and communications in 1919 were primitive, as experienced by this ranger.
—U.S. Forest Service

Lookouts have become quite modern, sometimes even including television. "We are experiencing audio difficulties. Please do not adjust your set."

A trail blaze on a tree

Map tables on lookouts can be used to pick out surrounding peaks.

hundred-foot spire in Glacier National Park which had never been climbed fell over and doesn't even exist any more. Beartooth Mountain, north of Helena, lost its tooth in 1878. No climbing guide can eliminate your responsibility to mesh available information with current field conditions to create an efficient climbing effort.

Trails: There are man-made trails (usually called pack trails), and there are game trails. Man-made trails are the ones drawn on maps. (A few trails built by hunters are not usually mapped.) They are excavated out of the terrain, and timber is removed with axes and saws. Switchbacks, which you shouldn't cut across, are common. Above timberline, these trails are often marked by cairns. In timber, they are blazed: the trees are marked with an axe to show the route, and they can be followed over the snow. Blazes are made on both sides of the tree and at the same height above the ground. If the blazes don't match on both sides, they are probably natural scars. One should be careful because section lines located by surveyors are also blazed, the difference being that survey lines have a single long blaze, while trail blazes consist of a long blaze with a short blaze above. They are sometimes highlighted with paint (usually orange). In time these blazes grow over but can still be recognized by seams in the bark filled with pitch. Blazes are helpful in following old trails which have faded due to disuse, blowdown, or lack of maintenance. Game trails are unmarked paths which can be very useful, although they often go from nowhere in particular to a similar place.

Map Use: The two most common types of maps are U.S. Forest Service National Forest maps and U.S. Geological Survey topographic maps. Bureau of Land Management maps similar to National Forest maps cover the eastern two-thirds of the state. Topographic map coverage is available for every spot in the state, with much of the coverage being in the extremely useful 7½' format of 2.6 inches to the mile. On them, one can carefully measure between two known points within 20' of accuracy. National Forest maps are available from any Forest Service office, and Bureau of Land Man-

Ducks are small cairns which you can build to mark your route.

Cairns are used to mark a trail above timberline or across meadows

16

U.S. GOVERNMENT OFFICES
—Sources of Public Maps—

Area	Main Office	Offices where maps are also available
U.S. Forest Service Region 1	Federal Building — P.O. Box 7669 Missoula, MT 59807 (406) 329-3511	(This office carries all National Forest maps.)
Beaverhead National Forest	P.O. Box 1258 Dillon, MT 59725 (406) 683-3900	Wisdom — Ennis Wise River Sheridan
Bitterroot National Forest	316 N. 3rd St. Hamilton, MT 59840 (406) 363-3131	Sula — West Fork Stevensville Darby
Custer National Forest	P.O. Box 2556 Billings, MT 59103 (406) 657-6361	Red Lodge — Fort Howes Ashland — Ekalaka Camp Crook (S. Dak.)
Deerlodge National Forest	P.O. Box 400 Butte, MT 59703 (406) 496-3400	Deerlodge Whitehall Philipsburg
Flathead National Forest	P.O. Box 147 Kalispell, MT 59901 (406) 755-5401	Bigfork — Whitefish Hungry Horse — Condon Columbia Falls
Gallatin National Forest	P.O. Box 130 Bozeman, MT 59715 (406) 587-6700	Big Timber — Gardiner Livingston — Cooke City West Yellowstone — Squaw Creek
Helena National Forest	Drawer 10014 Helena, MT 59626 (406) 449-5201	Lincoln Townsend
Kootenai and Kaniksu National Forest	506 US 2 West Libby, MT 59923 (406) 293-6211	Fortine — Eureka Sylvanite — Troy Canoe Gulch — Trout Creek
Lewis & Clark National Forest	P.O. Box 871 Great Falls, MT 59403 (406) 727-0901	Augusta — Choteau Neihart — Stanford Harlowton — White Sulphur Springs
Lolo National Forest	Fort Missoula — Bldg. 24 Missoula, MT 59801 (406) 329-3750	Superior — Seeley Lake Plains — Thompson Falls Ninemile (Huson)
Bureau of Land Management State Office	P.O. Box 36800 Billings, MT 59107 (406) 657-6561	(The Bureau recommends all map requests be submitted to the state office)
Butte District Bureau of Land Management	P.O. Box 3388 Butte, MT 59702 (406) 494-5059	Dillon Missoula
Lewistown District Bureau of Land Management	Airport Road Lewistown, MT 59457 (406) 538-7461	Great Falls Malta — Havre Glasgow
Miles City District Bureau of Land Management	P.O. Box 940 Miles City, MT 59301 (406) 232-4331	
Glacier National Park	West Glacier, MT 59936 (406) 888-5441	All park entrances and visitors' centers

An approach strategy is the most important ingredient needed to make a climb enjoyable.

Krummholz is timber growing along the ground in alpine areas, where it is regularly savaged by the weather. It takes its hostilities out on climbers who try to find an easy way through.

agement maps at any Bureau of Land Management office. The U.S. Forest Service maps sometimes have topographic map indexes on them for the area they cover. Topographic maps can be purchased in various sporting goods stores in larger towns, or you can order them from the U.S. Geological Survey, Federal Center, Building 41, Denver, Colorado 80225. These maps are also available for inspection and photocopying in major libraries. The Forest Service has recently come out with some new maps of selected areas which show National Forest information over a topographic base. They also have a new series of maps called Forest Travel Plans. These are up-to-date and show all new roads, along with current road restrictions and closures. When you call, write, or stop by a Forest Service office for current road and trail information, be sure to ask for one of these handy maps, which cost $1.00.

Trails are occasionally poorly located on National Forest maps. These mistakes are not widespread, but seem to occur in clusters in certain areas. Roads shown on lands adjacent to National Forests are also sometimes wrong. Get the most recent map, since the Forest Service has corrected some of the mistakes on previous editions. Topographic maps, especially more recent ones, usually have trails located exactly, but a few aren't even close. Whatever map you use, always believe the map until you have determined it is definitely in error.

Private Access: Approaches to many peaks in central and eastern portions of the state are across private land. National Forest and Bureau of Land Management maps show where the public and private land is, and often indicate where you might locate the landowner. It is of course common sense and courtesy to get permission to cross private land; it's also against the law to trespass. Getting permission is also a great way to get route advice, and sometimes keys to locked gates.

General Approach Strategy: For most climbs, the difficult and unpleasant part is to get to timberline, where the fun begins. Allow plenty of time to rest, gawk, take pictures, snack, and soak sore feet. Consider the habitat carefully. Unless you have a defined trail, stay out of brushy creek bottoms. Seek open, south-facing slopes. An ascending ridge with a southwest exposure (facing southwest) is ideal. North ridges and slopes tend to be choked with vegetation and downfall. In northwestern Montana, the major ranges usually have a steep west side where direct ascents can be made. Eastern approaches are more broken up. They may be safer and not as steep, but are circuitous and more irritating.

When climbing loose rock slopes, try to avoid the looser rock and seek bedrock for better footing. When descending, stay in the scree and lean a little forward, not back. This gives more control and puts the weight down on your feet, not outward. This technique also works well higher up if you are running down a scree slope, where

A climber provides protection for his partner with a belay. Note that the belayer is anchored to a large flake of rock behind him, and his body is braced.

hopping down with the feet turned a little to the side, if done carefully, is great sport.

Snowfields and Glaciers: You can encounter snowfields quite often. Sometimes you can just walk across them. You'll want to kick steps in the moderately sloped ones, and perhaps carry two long pointed rocks in your hands for snow daggers in the event of a slip. If you plan to do much climbing, you should get an ice axe and learn to use it. No matter how good you become with the ax, try to avoid sections where the snowfield below you ends abruptly in rocks or a precipice.

Steep-angle snowfields and glaciers require use of a rope and crampons. Crampons are frames of steel spikes which fit on the bottom of your boots. Ropes are things you never step on while wearing crampons. Traveling alone on glaciers isn't discussed here because it's stupid.

Basic Rockcraft: On bare rock, the fundamental climbing technique, regardless of your skill or the route's difficulty, is the Three-Point Stance, which means you always keep three of your four limbs in place, providing stability while allowing your free arm or leg to make the next move or explore the situation. If one point fails, you are still held to the rock by the other two.

When the route is exposed, a rope is necessary. Proper belaying makes a rope a safety device. Otherwise it is a lethal hazard to everyone on it. Know and practice the Belay Elements of Friction, Position, and Anchor. You can develop your technique by practice, climbing with knowledgeable friends, or attending a climbing school. Established climbing schools are located in the nearby Tetons and Cascades.

Running down a scree slope, an immediate reward to a completed ascent. —Cal Tassinari

A climber rappels using a friction device fashioned from carabiners.

—Kalispell Weekly News

Young climbers learn all the moves on a boulder, where conditions are fairly safe and opportunities for fun are endless.

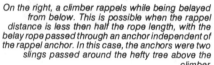

On the right, a climber rappels while being belayed from below. This is possible when the rappel distance is less then half the rope length, with the belay rope passed through an anchor independent of the rappel anchor. In this case, the anchors were two slings passed around the hefty tree above the climber.

For more detailed information on rock climbing, the booklet *Basic Rockcraft* by Royal Robbins is a good way to pick up the fundamentals. Another book, *The Freedom of the Hills* by Ed Peters is an extensive examination of mountaineering in general and is also recommended. There is plenty of literature available on snow and ice technique. These books, along with state-of-the-art climbing gear, can be found in mountain sports stores in all of Montana's major cities. These stores have only recently begun to stock this equipment, and here it is possible to completely outfit yourself for a serious expedition. You are encouraged to buy your climbing equipment locally so that these outlets can continue to offer a full line of quality gear.

What To Take: Although climbing conditions vary greatly, standard equipment used in other places works well. For snow climbing, an ice axe is essential. Ice screws are useful mostly on waterfalls, but flukes can be applied in snow and ice slopes. Crampons are not needed on peaks climbed by the easiest route, but there are plenty of exciting variants where they are necessary. For rock climbing, nylon webbing made into slings can do wonders in sedimentary formations. Foxheads, and sometimes hexcentrics work well on igneous routes, with bongs and pitons used occasionally. Bolts are seldom used and are scarce in local climbing shops. The new tri-cams are available, however, and are well suited for both decomposed rock and rock-ice protection.

Outside of technical work, you may consider sturdy running shoes rather than hiking boots if your route goes directly from a trail to easy rock or alpine tundra. You will lose ankle support and will have to be careful, but you can travel faster and scramble more efficiently without heavy boots. For scree slopes or any snow work, you need hard-soled boots.

Other gear is pretty much your personal preference. As a minimum, consider *always* taking the following:

—Wind-proof clothing, preferably waterproof.
—Map
—Water

Other important items are:

—Food
—Extra food
—Compass
—Waterproof matches

—Flashlight
—Hat
—First Aid Kit
—Gloves

Wildland Considerations: Camping in some regions is a simple affair, with lots of firewood and shelter material handy. In alpine areas, Glacier National Park, and various wildernesses, one should practice minimum impact camping. Bring a tent and gas stove, and camp back from trails, streams, lakes, and overused areas. Minimize disturbance of areas with thin or wet soil. Pack out your litter. You will find that Montanans have been quite litter conscious. When traveling cross-country in the timber, you may want to mark your return route with plastic survey flagging available from engineering supply outlets. In wilderness and other scenic areas, consider using crepe paper instead, as it will serve just as well and then decompose in a matter of days. Above timberline, you can mark your route with ducks, which are small stacks of rocks placed in conspicuous spots.

Respect all wildlife, large and small. Avoid disturbing eagle nesting sites which you may encounter on rock crags.

Colonies of ladybugs cluster on the rocks right on the summits when the sun is out. They seem to shun even the high ridges and are usually found only on the summits, sometimes carpeting the rocks there by the thousands.

A triangulation station

A benchmark

21

Old lookout buildings are fairly common and are as much a part of the history of the mountains as rocks themselves. These structures are protected under the Antiquities Act, and you should take care not to desecrate them. (Heavy fines are allowed under this Act, and there have been convictions.) Other government property and communications facilities are likewise covered by law. Survey markers such as benchmarks (vertical control points) and triangulation stations (horizontal control points), usually in the form of brass caps cemented onto stones, are also illegal to disturb. One should also consider that these were placed by cragsmen who clawed their way up these mountains back when they were a week's journey from anywhere, and then went down and passed away before we were born. Brass caps aren't souvenirs, and certainly shouldn't be offensive to wilderness purists. There's an aluminum tripod on Mt. Everest and a flag on the moon. Let the little brass disks serve as monuments to another breed of explorer.

Registers have been placed on many of Montana's summits, a number of them by the Forest Service. Recently this agency has done a complete turnabout on registers in wilderness areas, finding that registers are in conflict with wilderness management. Registers are now considered a structure, and the policy is to remove them when encountered. Be that as it may, this policy could backfire. The register on Granite Peak in the Beartooths has already been removed, and since the popularity of this summit makes questionable its "wilderness" quality anyway, the register will probably be replaced with all kinds of containers, grafitti engraved on rocks, and other memorabilia.

A few hotshot climbers don't like registers, and have taken it upon themselves to bring down or throw off registers in non-wilderness areas. For many people, climbing a mountain is one of the few things they will ever do to get a sense of accomplishment. It's a small thing to leave a register in place so that simple folk can sign it and leave their comments in it for the wind, God, and other climbers to read.

Technical Climbing Characteristics: Although any technical experience gained elsewhere is appropriate, there is no automatic transition to Montana rock. It is for patient climbers with a willingness to both explore and retreat. There is an entirely different kind of skill used to climb sloppy rock, and one must develop local tricks-of-the-trade.

Montana has no perfect rock, but a lot of fairly good rock. The nearby Wind Rivers, Tetons, Bugaboos, and Cascades all have better rock. Yosemite has clean slabs with straight cracks. Here you'll find none of that. The Bitterroots are decomposed and have rounded cracks with pronounced frost shattering. The Beartooths are old exposed rock, quite variable, heavily weathered, and usually lacking classic, clean lines. Protection is difficult, and loose rock often compounds the problems. Young solid granite such as is found in the Boulder Batholith is prone to sluffing. And those are just the major igneous areas. The qualities of the more common limestone and shale formations vary greatly. Though these rocks are often better than the sedimentary rocks on popular climbs in the

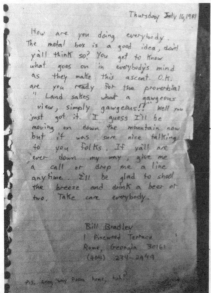

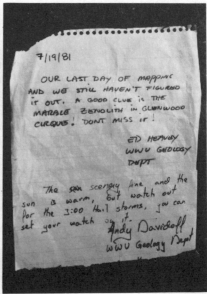

Registers can be considered the frosting on your summit cake.

Canadian Rockies, you often, as J. Gordon Edwards says in his Glacier National Park guide, "have to hold the mountain together while you climb it." Luckily, the vertical pitches are a little bit firmer than the massive sloping scree mountains they are interspersed with. Then, of course, there are the useless sandstone formations scattered around on the prairie, and the limestone spires in the Big Belt Mountains which fall over when you look at them sideways. Even in the granitic ranges, there are 2000' vertical walls so rotten they aren't elaborated on in this book.

Montana's Technical Climbing Ethics: In the 1960s and 1970s, when technical climbing here was getting its start, climbers here became concerned about the possible exploitation and degradation of their favorite backyard crags. To be sure, there was some hush-hush elitism involved by those who merely wanted no one but themselves to use the areas. Nonetheless, a genuine concern has since taken shape that these unique areas could lose their unspoiled character with a handle given for every move on every cliff and spire, and a profusion of ratings and dotted lines turning the wild faces into skill museums. Local climbers experience simple enjoyment and feel no need to prove anything to the rest of the rock climbing community. So, if you come to Montana to enjoy the unspoiled nature of the local formations and are interested in learning about or exploring areas outside the limelight which have been treated with respect, you would certainly be welcome.

Most Montana technicians agree on three things, agreements reached indepen-

Approaching a granite roof using direct aid
—Marvin McDonald collection

dently by local climbers living up to 500 miles apart. Please consider these ethics carefully:

1. Find out what's going on in a given area. The major areas are generally climbed clean. (Example: In the Boulder Batholith, the Humbugs are climbed as clean as possible, but the Homestake area has short blank faces where bolts are occasionally tried.) Usually, bolts are used sparingly, if at all. There is more emphasis on climbing clean than on climbing free, reflecting the attitude that pride in keeping a route pristine is equal to or exceeds pride in making a climb without direct aid. It's far better to hang etriers from a fox head than to make a free move protected by a bolt.

2. Carefully consider material submitted for publication. Articles giving detailed descriptions of routes, extensive decimal ratings, dotted line diagrams, cosmic route names, and other such yosemitization are not really appropriate, although sometimes descriptions of basic or popular routes are written and photocopied for local use. Old routes, new route variants, direct variants, free climbs of aid pitches, first ascents, and other such topics are of little concern. Articles which describe the fun, courage, and adventure of climbing a generally unspecified route would probably be quite interesting and well received.

3. Remember the prevailing method or first ascent principle. Try not to insist on doing a popular route as pure as possible, chopping out bolts and handholds as you go. On the other hand, installing superfluous permanent hardware is not so good either. Being in harmony with the rock means you can be in harmony with those who have been there before you, and those who are to follow.

Warning to Mountaineers

The mountains do not respect experience.

You have nothing to fear but no fear itself. If your fear isn't loud enough for you to hear, you cannot climb safely, because each move must be made with the thorough confidence generated from extreme care and awareness of all your options.

Sooner or later, you can expect to find yourself in situations you never would have encountered if you had used normal common sense. It is then you find self-reliance. When you get out of these situations, it isn't luck. It's your skill and judgment and personal strength and magic. But climbers seldom boast very loudly about this, because they know they develop wisdom as they become entangled in situations through their own underlying stupidity.

Your stupidity and danger are there for all to see. Your enlightenment and personhood are your secret. If you get wrapped up in your secret and forget there can be something unconsciously suicidal in your love of the mountains, there's a heavy price to pay. Many of the world's most accomplished mountaineers have died on their beloved mountains.

When you stand on any summit, you are looking down on a beautiful planet, where you live. May you continue to do so.

An injured climber is evacuated from the upper reaches of Granite Peak in the Beartooths.
—Rick Reese

I Told You So

"One of the inalienable freedoms of the mountains is the freedom to turn back whenever the margin of safety seems to be getting too thin, to know that the mountain will still be there tomorrow."

—David Brower

Climbing accidents that happen to others seem to be far-off remote occurrences. When one happens to you, that feeling of remoteness is magnified in all its more miserable aspects. These accidents are attributable to a variety of causes. Technical rock climbs have the obvious danger of exposure, but most climbing accidents in Montana result from more subtle dangers, and from simple carelessness or ignorance.

Loose Rock: This is typical of nearly every range in Montana, and especially treacherous in Glacier National Park and adjacent ranges. Here ledges are often covered with ball-bearing shale which slides out underneath your feet. Remove loose rock from handholds and footholds. "Firm up" your steps by allowing your feet to settle in before placing your full weight on them.

Wet Rock: Much of the rock in Montana is smooth sedimentary material which has virtually no traction when wet. Impending rain on a route requiring friction technique is reason enough to retreat, as delayed descent may be impossible. Waterfalls, even small ones, are always to be respected.

Falling Rock: Rockfall is usually triggered by climbers on moderate slopes. Climb diagonally on a slope so you aren't exposed to rock kicked loose by a friend directly above you. If this isn't practical, take turns moving while the resting climbers wait in sheltered locations, or stay in a tight group. Be extra alert in chutes and gulleys. Rocks bounce erratically, so if you are caught in the open and can't get safely out of the line of fire, watch a falling rock until it is near you, then evade it. Careful climbers shouldn't

Corniced snowdrifts look solid from above, but can collapse should you walk out on them.

When in central and eastern Montana, watch out for the Easily-rattled, Double-fanged Handhold Nullifier.

knock any rocks loose, but if you do dislodge one, yell "Rock!" immediately to alert the others, even if you aren't sure whether or not the rock is going to take off.

Natural forces can set rock loose on vertical routes, where helmets should be used.

Snowfields: These are often encountered, especially early in the season. You should always have an ice axe along, even if the climb doesn't warrant crampons or ropes, as an axe will help you keep your balance to prevent slipping in the first place. Injuries and fatalities from sliding down snowfields have been common in Montana. Avoid steep snowfields if possible, especially if you can't see the run-out. Wear sturdy boots to kick steps. Never go out on a snow slope where you aren't confident of your ability to self-arrest. Avoid crevasses (where you should be roped up anyway), low sumps which have a wet or icy appearance, and areas where you can hear running water underneath.

Cornices: These are another deadly snow hazard. Cornices are huge dunes of snow which form on ridgetops. The warm wind blowing up a slope curls around the cornice and hollows out the leeward side, forming an overhang which can collapse under your weight. Staying well back from the edge is a simple and effective precaution.

Avalanches: Some areas of the state have avalanche forecasts on the radio during the winter. Factors of temperature, snow stratification, and wind all play a part in the development of avalanche conditions. Large cornices on ridges above you, well developed avalanche chutes, and the snow crust "slabbing" as you cross an area are easily visible indicators of danger. High slopes and bowls are also suspect, leaving ridgetops as the preferred approach routes on a winter climb. If you suspect avalanche danger, the best advice is to be scared to death and leave the area quietly. Montana's worst climbing tragedy, where five climbers died on Mt. Cleveland in Glacier National Park in 1969, was the result of an avalanche.

Boulder Fields: The first thing one notices about these areas is that the stones are not neatly stacked. Short falls can easily result in injuries and a very difficult evacuation. No rock, regardless of size, can be assumed to be set firmly in place.

Lightning: You can encounter dangerous electrical conditions with no warning other than stormy-looking clouds. Early warning signals are funny crackling noises, hair standing on end, and far-off lightning activity. When lightning strikes a peak, it breaks up to disperse its charge over the entire vicinity. If on a peak or exposed ridge when lightning is imminent, get off immediately, with a crouching run if the terrain permits. Sometimes storms pass quickly, and it may not be necessary to abandon the climb, but you must wait it out somewhere, and that is taking a calculated risk. Caves and overhangs are nice because they're dry, but are not necessarily safe. There have been lightning fatalities in caves. Search for a dry sheltered spot well below the exposed ridge or summit. Avoid gullies where the rain water will wash down, as you are certain to be zapped there if a strike does occur anywhere above. Once you have selected a spot, squat on your toes without touching any rock with your hand or body, or sit on dry insulating material from inside your pack. This way you do not provide your body as a

Grizzly bears go to the summits on hot days. Here a couple are standing by the summit cairn of Rising Wolf Mountain in Glacier National Park.

path for electric current. If you are committed to a technical route, tie in on a short rope or sling, unclip from the climbing rope, and stand on one foot or (preferably) dangle. These are good techniques if you are caught in a spot, but it is worth emphasizing that avoiding the threat of lightning entirely is the only action that is unequivocably recommended.

Hypothermia: This is a cooling of the inner body temperature caused by blustery conditions coupled with exhaustion and/or inadequate clothing. Symptoms are shivering, speech problems, lack of coordination, and drowsiness. The best prevention is to watch the weather and your companions. Treatment is to get the victim out of the rain and wind, then get him/her dry and warm by any means available (fire, body heat). Be sure to keep the victim awake, and serve up hot drinks.

Altitude Sickness: This is not very common at elevations found in Montana, but it can be a factor above 9000' and has caused fatalities at that elevation. General symptoms are nausea, dizziness, headache, and breathing problems. Descent is the only cure, but sometimes recovery can be made quickly enough to resume climbing. The best prevention for altitude sickness is to take your time and not overexert yourself. Drink plenty of fluids, as the thin dry air draws off body moisture rapidly, and dehydration contributes to altitude sickness.

There are three kinds of altitude sickness, though the symptoms often overlap. *Acute Mountain Sickness* consists of headache, loss of appetite, nausea, vomiting, weakness, and shortness of breath. It will sometimes pass with a little aspirin, lots of fluids, and easy activity around camp. If it gets worse, descend. *Pulmonary Edema* is an accumulation of water in the lungs. Shortness of breath, and coughing with frothy pink sputum indicates emergency descent is required, as the patient's condition can deteriorate rapidly. *Cerebral Edema* is an accumulation of water around the brain. It is not a common form of altitude sickness but is very serious. Symptoms are severe headache, hallucinations, and impaired speech and movement. The brain becomes retarded in its ability to run the functions of the body. Treatment is immediate descent.

Tent Fires: Shelter can be critical when camping up high, and cooking or running a stove for warmth inside a tent is not encouraged. Tent quarters are usually cramped, and one false move can result in severe burns from either fire or boiling water. Burn victims are often in too much pain to move and require a litter or helicopter evacuation. (Mountain helicopter evacuations aren't safe, either, and have resulted in the loss of life and machine in the Beartooths.) Cook outside. Build a rock shelter for the stove if it's windy.

Time: Time waits for no man, and that goes double for mountaineers. The difficulties of descending in darkness are legendary. More often, lack of time pressures one to hurry, take unnecessary risks, and lose one's way. ANYONE can get lost. The simple enjoyment of the climb is diminished. Also, arriving on the summit early in the day greatly reduces the chances of encountering lightning problems.

Vicious Beasts: Precautions to take in bear country include making noise when you travel, leaving your dog at home, keeping a clean camp with trees nearby you can climb, and avoiding the creatures when sighted. Yellowstone National Park recommends traveling in groups of at least four people. Bear danger is highest in Glacier National Park and the Mission Range. Danger is also noteworthy in the Cabinet, Purcell, Bitterroot, Swan, Flathead, and Rocky Mountain Front ranges. The southern portion of the Absaroka and Gallatin ranges are also places to take bear precautions. If you are aggressively confronted by a bear, and are pursued when trying to back away slowly, you have the choice of either climbing a tree or playing dead. If you opt for a handy tree, shed your pack, which may distract the bear. You should keep a loop in the strap which goes through the buckle of your hip belt so that you can release it quickly. If you play dead, curl up in a ball, hands over the back of your neck, with your pack on to provide some protection.

Moose are not to be taken lightly, and have been known to defend their young from grizzly bears. The best defense is to simply not invade their space. They aren't as ungainly as they look. They avoid man as much out of annoyance as fear, and will pursue you only if they feel you are instigating a threat. Once pursued, instigators better find a tree. The animal isn't bluffing, and means to stomp you.

These are guidelines to help you, not laws of nature. The only rule is, try not to panic. Attempt to vibe out the creature you are facing, and give it a chance to vibe you out. Be as friendly and unobtrusive as you can. You are confronting a wild and intelligent creature who should have the opportunity to think the same of you.

Water: Most water in the higher mountains above timberline is OK to drink. Below timberline there may be giardia, a treacherous little organism whose purpose in life is to scuttle your digestive tract. It is common in many locations, and you would do well to boil or otherwise treat your drinking water. Also, many mountainous areas are grazed. Cattle seem to delight in fouling water sources.

The Cow: Nature's ultimate search and destroy unit of mountain drinking water.

Alcohol, Tobacco, & "Other Substances": These can impair your judgment and strength more than usual at high altitude or when tired. No matter what advertisers suggest, there's a better high awaiting you at the summit if you just go the way God made you. Granted, many climbers have their own favorite habits of celebrating on top, but these activities should be tempered with the realization that you still have to get down off the thing. You're in enough trouble as it is. Please use care and discretion appropriate to what you are climbing.

Solo Climbing: Going alone is not necessarily dangerous in itself, but it is a calculated risk depending on the nature of the climb. It has its own rewards, and you can go anytime you want, but you reduce your hazards when you go with someone else. When your friend makes the top, your own victory is doubled.

Attitude: Serious climbing is a team effort, and a fine thing to do with friends. The self-important attitudes prevalent in the "me" generation have no place in a team effort and are as terrifying as any natural hazard. The important thing is for the more experienced climbers to work and share with the novices the skill, knowledge, and patience the mountains have endowed upon them.

Incompetence: A group of climbers is incompetent when the sum total of their combined knowledge and experience is not sufficient to solve the problems they are likely to encounter. Very few otherwise proficient climbers have the self-rescue skills necessary for their more serious endeavors, and they accept this lack as a fundamental risk of climbing. It isn't. Climbing at the edge of confidence but no further is a thrilling wisdom to develop, as well as a responsible attitude. Such a climber can then serve to help those who are still learning this valuable lesson.

Some local law enforcement agencies are not well set up to deal with mountain rescues. Let the local authorities know if you are willing to assist in a rescue.

Wildland Management:
An Essay for Climbers

"We do not have an energy crisis; we have a crisis in government management."
—James Watt

It took billions of years for the Montana landscape to be shaped into what it is today, and in a few short years we are deciding what to do with it. Although the land has many values, our system of resource allocation is based on worth to humans, and if an area is not used and/or appreciated by a healthy number of voters, its wilderness or recreational value is diminished and it is only proper under our system to open the area to more exploitive types of interests.

The total climbing experience is shaped by the way the land is managed. It may take a full day of hard travel on foot just to get to the base of one remote mountain, while one can drive a car to the top of another some afternoon. Both ascents are positive enjoyable experiences. The circumstances of each can, by comparison, enhance the enjoyment of the other. Either way, the mountains don't need preservation. They are monuments to the building up and tearing down of the earth's crust. They form and preserve themselves by destruction. In the process their summits provide striking views and new perspectives, regardless of what man has done below. Without climbers, a valuable expression of this wild and precious resource would not occur. Climbers are knowledgeable hikers, backpackers and campers as a necessay part of their craft. They are also generally tough-minded people and can often overlook their own personal biases. They belong at the forefront of the political scene, speaking out for appropriate wildland use.

Recreational overuse is a problem, but it is not *the* problem. The problem is concentration of use which produces a high impact on choice portions of the wildland resource, use which can be widely dispersed. Where wildland visitors don't encounter anyone else during their trips, it means that all that beauty spends most of its time all by itself, just waiting to be appreciated. There are trails carved out of the mountains' flanks that are overgrown from disuse. Now other land interests are attempting to weasel into

A peak just west of Tabletop Mountain in the Highland Mountains. Note the small mine prospect which is supplied by helicopter. Operations such as this one by Exxon have a much smaller environmental impact than the old bulldozer operations. Mountaineers should continue to press for environmental safeguards in these types of activities, and also appreciate when mining companies have gone the extra mile to minimize impacts.

East Rosebud Lake. The Beartooth Wilderness boundary is at the far side of the lake. Heavy recreational use was already established here when the wilderness was designated.
—U.S. Forest Service

areas that seem to be unused and unappreciated. With these new demands, saving an area for future generations is no longer an adequate argument. The future is here, and we are the generation looking at all the alternatives.

We are worried about the quality of our wilderness fantasies while other interests are zeroing in on our wildlands with legal realities and political expertise. Beware the Wilderness Fanatic syndrome—a personality trait which lives to one degree or another in all of us who love the outdoors. The Wilderness Fanatic misses how the West was before Lewis and Clark, mopes around in the wilderness areas, and never tells anybody where he's been or what he's seen. He's the environmentalist who wants to keep some beautiful place a secret on the off chance that he may want to spend an afternoon there ten years later without seeing anybody. He advocates Wildland Hoarding, the setting aside for wilderness of every roadless acre, the locking up of the national resources which under our system of government do belong to the people. He's even offended on a summit by a survey marker or register, and removes it. He's seen as a selfish elitist, giving environmentalism and the wilderness ethic a bad name.

Wilderness designation will not solve all our land management problems. The wilderness concept is a wonderful ideal, but ideals mean nothing if one ignores the problems that go hand in hand with them. For one thing, the core wilderness areas we now have were designated before it was economically desirable to exploit them. They were not designated because they represented a cross-section of how things used to be on this continent. They were designated because they were the last, most rugged, God-forsaken miserable deserted middles-of-nowhere we had. (From 1898 to 1907, Tom Danaher had a ranch in what is now the Bob Marshall Wilderness. Things got tough and he moved on. If he had made a go of it, others would have come in, and today there would be no Bob.) We respect these areas because up till now they have been too tough for us, not because they represent the harmony of nature unaltered by man. That's why people expect designated wilderness areas to be rather stark, remote chunks of acreage. They don't expect plains where cattle graze, or low rolling hills, even though in their unroaded state such places are by definition unaltered by man.

Another problem with wilderness designation is that it doesn't work too well once substantial numbers of people start concentrating in key areas. The designation itself may encourage people, especially wilderness fantasists, to thumb their noses at their backyard wildlands and flock to the designated wilderness areas. The East Rosebud drainage in the Beartooth Wilderness is a good example of an area so popular and accessible that wilderness designation seems inappropriate. Granite Peak, just west of there, is wild, rugged and exhilarating. But these very qualities plus its status as the state's highest peak have attracted much use, diminishing the area's "wilderness" qualities as defined by management guidelines. Making a wilderness and then pretending people won't be interested in going there any more is an application of the maxim that, "If the facts do not conform to the theory, they must be disposed of."

Wilderness is an extreme method of preservation because by definition it excludes nearly all practical uses. This means the more wilderness areas you have, the more difficult it is to justify managing them as such. The resources "locked up" in wilderness areas are seen in the aggregate, not as individual deposits in each area. Also, overuse disputes continually confront the wilderness manager, who must enforce this relative term. Some would consider a Vibram print on a lakeshore to be overuse. Others would suggest a paving job around the lake would prevent such overuse. For wilderness to survive, it must do so without exceptions. The "purist" approach must prevail over what is "practical." Backcountry areas which aren't designated for wilderness should not be converted into wilderness unless they are so unique as to already have considerable public support. Wilderness areas must not be cheapened by having too many of them. Like national parks, they must be few, unique, and inviolate.

When special interest groups polarize wildland issues, public deception results. When the truth is discovered, deception turns into mistrust and resentment. As long as these groups war against each other, responsible officials will be caught in the crossfire, unable to provide acceptable solutions and receiving only blame. To answer the "resource crisis" deception, the resources locked up in current wilderness areas aren't adequate to carry this country through any kind of crisis period. The crisis is just the excuse the corporate interests use. To the "wilderness is best" deception, it's been pointed out here that wilderness is difficult to manage and excludes many kinds of user-intensive activities. Thus the push to lock up more and more wildland has weakened acceptance and support for the fine wilderness areas we already have, and has often left preservation groups licking their wounds. On the other hand, the push to open up our prime wilderness areas has made corporate prospectors appear to be insatiable engines of wildland destructon.

Wilderness, backcountry, mined and logged areas must be used by enlightened recreationists who respect the natural order of things and then return and speak out for the experienced tangible values they find, such as rejuvenation of body and spirit, as well as material products. Wildlands are no longer just for the recluse, the escapist, the fantasist. They belong to the constituency which is strong and determined enough to defend the values reaped there. We need a constituency that thinks positively, can see value and beauty in both a clearcut and an unlogged drainage, will document all the uses, can discuss intelligent trade-offs, and doesn't expect the battle to ever end.

There are some valuable precedents suggesting what could be done. Glacier National Park is visited by many people each year, yet it offers every type of wildland experience. Another established management option is to set aside pristine areas for light, dispersed low-impact recreation that would take pressure off designated wilderness areas. The Rattlesnake drainage north of Missoula is well placed and suited for extensive recreational use. Both a recreation and wilderness area were established there in 1980. The new Lee Metcalf Wilderness and adjacent Recreation Area, a product of compromise between previously warring special-interest groups, is a similar step in the right direction.

Besides setting up distinct areas, another approach would be to create new management designations similar to those in the Jewel Basin Hiking Area east of Kalispell and the Hyalite Canyon area south of Bozeman. Both these areas have relatively easy access, are very popular, and haven't been significantly altered by commercial activities. They provide excellent opportunities to see natural habitat and wildlife. They are readily available, regularly visited, sustain popular use in concurrence with their management designation, and sometimes have structures installed for visitor use. But as in wilderness areas, man is a visitor who does not remain. There are sunshine, wind, storms, beauty. All that's lacking are wilderness fanatics. The exhilaration and potential bred into those areas over billions of years remain unaltered.

Before wildland needs to be protected or exploited, it needs to be experienced. To experience it is to experience continued freshness of appreciation. Climbers do experience it, and should be politically active.

Blue Mountain Lookout overlooks commercial forest land north of Libby.

Looking north from Northwest Peak into Canada. USFS

Davis Mountain from trail on Northwest Peak. USFS

The Purcell Mountains

"I stayed on the hilltop in a state of ecstacy for what appeared to be an endless time, yet the whole event may have lasted only a few minutes, perhaps only as long as the sun shone before it reached the horizon."

—Carlos Castaneda

Description: A low-slung dispersion of forested ridgetops on gradual slopes, resembling a moderately dissected plateau, and surrounded by deep valleys. 5900' elevation span.

Geology: Precambrian sediments were exposed as the area uplifted and younger layers slid eastward to become the Whitefish Range and Glacier National Park.

Access: North of Libby. Forest roads from Highways 2 and 37 serve the entire area, with trails to the higher reaches.

Ownership: Kootenai National Forest.

■ **Northwest Peak 7705** [W] From Yaak drive two miles west on Highway 508. Turn right onto the Pete Creek Road, and stay on it for 13 miles. Take a left onto the West Fork Road. After two more miles, turn right onto the Winkum Creek Road. After seven miles on this road, watch for the signed trailhead on the left side, in an old logging unit. Head up the trail a couple miles to the peak, where you'll find an old lookout cabin.

Davis Mountain 7583 [S] East ridge. A longer, more scenic approach on the north ridge from Northwest Peak.

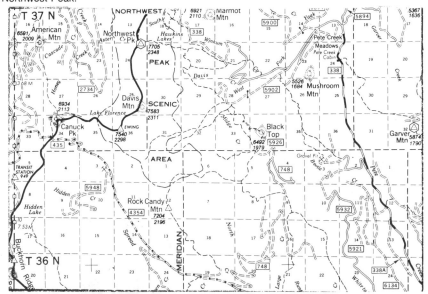

Gentle Mountains of the central Purcells.

The Mt. Baldy Lookout used to look like this, but has been replaced by a more modern structure. USFS

Canuck Peak 6934 [W] Old lookout tower and cabin.
Rock Candy Mountain 7204 [W] Old lookout site.
Keno Mountain 6542 [W] Old lookout site.
Mt. Baldy 6529 [P] Maintained lookout tower. Road not passable for cars.
Garver Mountain 5875 [W] Lookout tower.
Robinson Mountain 7539 [W] Cupola-style lookout cabin built in the 1920s, now available for overnight rental.
Newton Mountain 6538 [W] Old lookout site.
Clark Mountain 6418 [W]
Grizzly Point 6077 [W] Old lookout site.
Sheepherder Mountain 6409 [W]
Roderick Mountain 6644 [W] Old lookout building.
Mt. Henry 7243 [W] Old lookout tower.
Red Mountain 6599 [D] Old lookout site.
Boulder Mountain 7058 [W] Old lookout cabin.
Webb Mountain 5988 [D] Old lookout cabin, available for overnight rental.
Lost Horse Mountain 6559 [P] Short hike from end of road. Lookout tower built in 1934.

Top of Quartz Mountain
Francis Petit

Pink Mountain 6597 [W]

Pinto Point 5311 [W] Old lookout tower.

Yaak Mountain 4995 [P] Lookout tower built in 1958, still used.

Pulpit Mountain 6556 [W] Old lookout site.

King Mountain 5787 [P] Radio facilities.

O'Brien Mountain 6772 [W]

Quartz Mountain 6255 [W] Old steel lookout tower.

Turner Mountain 5952 [P] Ski lift to top. Old lookout site.

Mt. Tom 5827 [W]

Big Creek Baldy 5768 [P] Lookout tower and old cabin, available for rent year-round from the Forest Service. Call (406) 293-7741.

Parsnip Mountain 6161 [W] Timbered top. Lookout cabin built in 1914.

Lost Soul Mountain 6168 [W] Timbered summit.

Banfield Mountain 6100 [P] Old lookout site.

Ziegler Mountain 5394 [P] Maintained lookout.

■ **Blue Mountain 6040** [D] Take the Pipe Creek Road from Highway 37 on the north side of Libby and go six miles. A sign points out the Blue Mountain Road, which winds around some but has a good grade. Stay on the main road. Near the top, take the uphill fork of any unsigned junctions. At the top are various radio facilities, a lookout cabin (still in use) built in 1928, and a 72' steel tower.

Technical Opportunities: A fractured boulder or short cliff here and there. There are no significant crag areas, but the old steel lookout towers get pretty thrilling when the wind picks up.

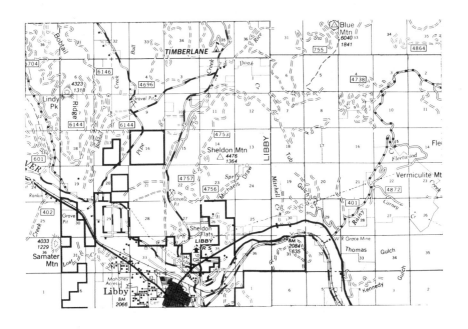

Looking east up Middle Fork of the Bull River. Left to right are A Peak, Snowshoe Peak (left of center) and Ibex Peak. Little Ibex Peak is on the northeast ridge of Ibex Peak, near center of picture.

Scenery Mountain Lookout
Francis

In the 1960s the old Keeler Mountain Lookout was replaced. The old tower was then torn down. Bob Lichlyter, courtesy of Lefty Young

The Cabinet Mountains

"Ye crags and peaks, I'm with you once again! . . .
O sacred forms, how proud you look!
How high you lift your heads into the sky!
How huge you are! how mighty and how free!

—James Sheridan Knowles

Description: An abrupt range with a 6900' elevation span. Thickly forested slopes, sometimes with brush jungles. Low base elevation and abundant precipitation often mean a vertical mile up to timberline, where the peaks become complex and heavily glaciated. Late melting snow accounts for many accidents—bring an ice axe.

Geology: Younger rock slid eastward to expose older rock, which lifted higher than the Purcells and was then more heavily glaciated.

Access: South of Libby. Highways 2, 200, 56, and the Thompson River Road serve numerous logging roads. Trails climb to the more rugged remote areas.

Ownership: Coeur d'Alene, Kootenai, and Lolo national forests.

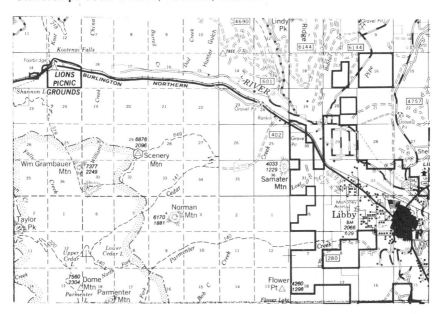

A Peak is connected to Snowshoe Peak (left) by a long ridge.

Snowshoe Peak from the east. Leigh Lake is hidden in the hanging valley. The northeast ridge crosses the photo and joins the summit ridge just left of the peak.

WEST OF HIGHWAY 56

Survey Mountain 6437 [S] Southeast ridge.

Burnt Peak 6300 [S] Northwest ridge. Old lookout building.

Keeler Mountain 4943 [J] Manned lookout tower. Old cabin.

Drift Peak 6342 [S] West ridge from Cheer Creek saddle.

Savage Mountain 6906 [S] East ridge.

Spar Peak 6585 [W] Old lookout site. A snow chute is a technical alternative.

Sawtooth Mountain 6763 [S] East side from South Fork of Ross Creek.

Billiard Table 6622 [S] Take a timbered spur from the mines to the west. Grass covered top.

Squaw Peak 6167 [W] Maintained lookout building. Stone lookout cabin built 1910. In 1907 this peak was the first forest lookout in Montana.

EAST OF HIGHWAY 56

Grambauer Mountain 7377 [W]

■ **Scenery Mountain 6876** [W] Find the Cedar Creek road on Highway 2, five miles west of Libby. Follow it 2½ miles to the end. Take the Cedar Creek trail for about ¾ mile to a trail junction (elevation 3400'). Take the right fork and climb 4½ miles to the top. The lookout is usually manned in the summer.

Dome Mountain 7560 [S] Short scramble from trail to the west.

Parmenter Mountain 7345 [S] Southeast approach.

Sugarloaf Mountain 7568 [S] South ridge from Sky lakes.

Treasure Mountain 7694 [S]

Mt. Snowy 7618 [S]

A Peak 8634 [S] Register. West face from North Fork of the Bull River, then up the west ridge. The summit can also be reached by a C-rated traverse on the ridge that connects it to Snowshoe Peak. There is some exposure—consider taking a rope. Halfway along, drop off the ridge at an obvious obstruction, then climb back on once past. The great north wall of A Peak is rotten and rated T. Just off this wall is a large pinnacle named Prester Tower, a C-rated climb up a series of ramps on its southeast side.

Snowshoe Peak 8738 [S] Register. West side, or a C-rated ascent via the northeast ridge. Go straight up from Leigh Lake to gain the ridge and its stunning views. Ice enthusiasts can approach on Blackwell Glacier.

Ibex Peak from the west. Little Ibex Peak is at the end of the northeast ridge.

Peak 7764 from the east, looking up Big Cherry Creek. Peak 7570 is just to the right.

St. Paul Peak and Chicago Peak (flat top) from the west.

Elephant Peak from the east.

Bockman Peak 8174 [S]

Ibex Peak 7676 [S] From the northwest. Often done as the first part of a Little Ibex Peak climb. Little Ibex, 7146', is at the end of the northeast ridge of Ibex and is T-rated. When traversing this exposed knife-edged ridge, drop down the northwest side to clear a notch. There is a register on Little Ibex and a plaque placed by the Spokane Mountaineers to commemorate a climbing instructor killed in a fall.

Lentz Peak 7298 [T] From the southeast.

Peak 7764 [S] One mile east of Lentz Peak. Best approached from the east.

Berray Mountain 6177 [W] Old lookout tower.

Bald Eagle Peak 7655 [S]

Lost Horse Mountain 5806 [S] Old lookout site.

St. Paul Peak 7714 [S] Northwest ridge from trail, or by traversing east side Chicago peak.

Chicago Peak 7018 [S] Interesting summit of rock tables separated by large clefts.

Rock Peak 7583 [S] East face has a chimney rated easy T.

Elephant Peak 7938 [S] East ridge. Other approaches T-rated. An ice chute on the Libby Creek side requires crampons. At the top of the chute is a chockstone rated C, done carefully.

Ojibway Peak 7303 [S] From the east. A T-rated route on the west face follows a crack system of good rock just left of the highest point.

Twin Peaks 7563 [S] East ridge. Jeep trails and old mine roads on Great Northern Mountain to the east.

Flat Top Mountain 7698 [S] Southeast ridge from Wanless Lake.

Carney Peak 7173 [S] Popular overlook reached from Carney Pass to the southeast.

Engle Peak 7583 [W] Trail from the west.

Goat Peak 6889 [S] West ridge from saddle reached by trail.

Green Mountain 5456 [W] Old lookout site. Accessible by trail or gated road.

Twenty Peak 6171 [W] High point on a long timbered ridgetop which extends southeast to Twenty Odd Peak, where there is an old lookout. A P-rated road approaches the top of Twenty Peak.

Silver Butte Mountain 6480 [S] Easy southwest ridge from trail on Canyon Peak.

Barren Peak 5365 [W] Old lookout tower built in 1934.

Jumbo Peak 5393 [S] Short climb up the north ridge to grassy top.

Allen Peak 6740 [W] Old lookout site. Jeep trail to radio facilities at 6231'.

Blacktail Peak 6103 [W]

Lost Horse Mountain

Wanless Lake with Engle Peak (left skyline), Goat Peak (left foreground), Flat Top Mountain (right skyline). —U.S. Forest Service

41

Twenty Peak and Twenty Odd Peak (right) from Noxon Reservoir to the southwest.

Cougar Peak (left) and Graves Peak from the south.

SOUTH OF THE VERMILLION RIVER

Seven Point Mountain 6660 [P] Lookout tower built 1930.
Cougar Peak 6694 [D] Maintained lookout buillding.
Graves Peak 7050 [W]
Vermillion Peak 6700 [S] Easy approach up the east ridge from good road through Vermillion Pass. Old lookout site on top.
Mt. Headley 7429 [W] Old lookout site.
Marmot Peak 7210 [W] Heliport site.
Cube Iron Mountain 7179 [W] Old lookout site.
Mt. Silcox 6854 [W] Old lookout site.
Priscilla Peak 7005 [W] Cupola-design lookout cabin.
Richards Peak 5771 [P] Manned lookout.

Cube Iron Mountain from the southwest.

Technical Opportunities: The Kootenai Falls area has rotten rock sometimes used for practice. The Bad Medicine area on the west side of Bull Lake has impressive cliffs and spires, also rotten. Smooth cirque headwalls are up the Middle Fork of Ross Creek. As for high endeavors on good rock, those opportunities don't really exist in the Cabinets. However, there is an abundance of sloping bedding planes scoured by glaciers, ideal for friction climbs. Generally, the steeper they are, the firmer the rock. Bald Eagle Peak, Cable Mountain, and Rock Peak are places where these slabs occur. Snow and ice climbs are also common, with snow chutes lasting well into the summer.

The Salish Mountains northwest from Meadow Peak. Calx Mountain on center skyline. Note small forest fire under the right skyline.

The Salish Mountains

"Great things are done when men and mountains meet."

—William Blake

Description: Forested hills and ridges with a 5000' elevation span. On the Flathead Reservation the hills are mostly grass-covered.

Geology: Sedimentary rocks over a billion years old were exposed and then faulted extensively as top layers slid eastward (like jello off a plate) into present-day Glacier National Park and the Bob Marshall Wilderness. Rocks in the Hog Heaven Hills area formed from a volcano 50 million years ago. More recently the small, grass-covered mountains on the Flathead Reservation were islands in glacial Lake Missoula. Shorelines and floodpaths are still visible.

Access: West of Kalispell, east of Libby. Highway 2 and several forest highways serve the major drainages. Trails to the high country start from logging roads in the smaller drainages.

Ownership: Kootenai, Lolo, and Flathead national forests, Flathead Indian Reservation.

NORTH OF HIGHWAY 2

Black Butte 4064 [D] Manned lookout tower.

Warex Point 6242 [W] Old lookout site.

McGuire Mountain 6991 [W] Cupola-style lookout cabin built in 1924, restored in 1983 and now available for overnight rental.

Pinkham Mountain 6322 [D] Old lookout tower.

Sunday Mountain 5485 [D] Old lookout site.

Warland Peak 5950 [W] 100' tall lookout tower built in 1935.

Davis Mountain 6053 [W] Old lookout tower.

Elk Mountain 6587 [W] Lookout cabin built in 1940.

Looking west from Swede Mountain—Libby (right), and the north end of the Cabinets

Sheppard Mountain 6216 [W]
Mt. Swamey 6349 [W]
Johnson Peak 6009 [W]Maintained lookout on a 90' steel tower.
Ingalls Mountain 6125 [W] Old lookout site.
Ashley Mountain 6297 [W] Old lookout site.
Swede Mountain 4305 [D] Manned lookout tower.
Tony Peak 4820 [P] Lookout tower built in 1934.
Richards Mountain 6005 [J] Old lookout site.
Calx Mountain 6550 [J] Old lookout site.
Kenelty Mountain 5931 [W] Lookout tower built in 1934.
■ **Meadow Peak 6709** [P] Turn off Highway 2 six miles west of the west end of MacGregor Lake onto the Lang Creek road. After 4½ miles the road will begin to climb out of Lang Creek. From there it's another six miles to the top. The last mile is rocky, and four-wheel drive will be useful on the last ¼ mile. During fire season there will usually be someone at the lookout to greet you.

SOUTH OF HIGHWAY 2

Murr Peak 6763 [W]
Castle Rock 6242 [W]
Bassoo Peak 6391 [J] Manned lookout building. Note: Access up Mill Creek to the east is usually restricted by the Flathead Tribe. Use trail approaching from the west.
Snowstorm Mountain 6992 [W] Old lookout site.

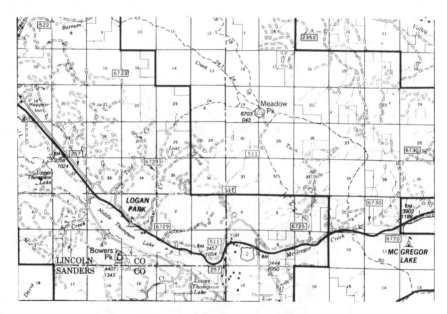

Murr Peak area from Meadow Peak. MacGregor Lake to the left

Lookout tower on Meadow Peak

Thompson Peak 7460 [W] Old lookout site.

Haskill Mountain 6290 [D] Maintained lookout.

Blacktail Mountain 6757 [D] Two-lane road to the top from Lakeside.

Hog Heaven Point 5277 [J] Old lookout site.

Irvine Point 5461 [J] Eighty-foot steel lookout tower.

Wild Horse Island 3745 [S] East approach from shoreline is shortest.

Big Arm Point 5176 [D] Old lookout site.

Big Hole Peak 6961 [W] Old lookout cabin on summit ridge at 6919'.

Baldy Mountain 7493 [W] Good trail up the northwest side. New lookout building on rounded summit.

Deemer Peak 6252 [J]

Oliver Point 4782 [D] Radio facility. West of Round Butte.

Round Butte 3422 [W] South approach from county road. Isolated hill west of Ronan on private land.

Schmitz Mountain 4958 [J] Old lookout site east of Hot Springs. Nearby ridges between Hot Springs and Ronan (around 5600') have ridgetop jeep trails.

Sonyok Mountain 5645 [J] Lookout building. Northwest of Dixon.

Red Sleep Mountain (High Point) 4885 [D] Lookout tower and cabin overlook National Bison Range.

Haskill Mountain from Smith Valley to the northeast

The old lookout tower on Blacktail Mountain was still in operation when the U.S. Air Force surrounded it with a radar site. The lookout hung a fluorescent tube near a window. Whenever radar lit the tube up, he had to go down and get a radiation check. The radar site has since been shut down, but the tower is still maintained.

Blacktail Mountain has more buildings than any other summit in Montana. Besides the lookout tower from where the picture was taken, there are a radar site, radio and telecommunications equipment, and a TV transmitter.

Baldy Mountain's southeast side   Schmitz Mountain from the northwest

Technical Opportunities: There are several practice areas near Kalispell. One is northwest of town on the Tally Lake Road, six miles from Tally Lake. Another is near the old dump on the northwest edge of Somers. A few cliffs west of Kila visible from Highway 2 are used for local climbing schools. The Somers and Kila formations are on private land, and permission is necessary to use them. As for all-day projects up in the mountains, there are none of real quality. There is a selection of crumbly sedimentary outcrops along the lower Thompson River. (Hint: Only the steepest ones aren't vegetated.) One may find enjoyable snowclimbs early in the summer. There is a nice chute which runs up from Baldy Lake into a notch on the south ridge of Baldy Mountain.

Technical climbing areas: Kila Cliffs (left), and uplifts at mouth of the Thompson River (right)

An abandoned lookout platform on Schley Mountain overlooks deep valleys.

The Coeur d'Alene Mountains

"Climbing to tranquility far above the cloud,
Conceiving the heavens clear of misty shroud,
Climb to tranquility, finding its real worth,
Conceiving the heavens flourishing on Earth."

—Graeme Edge

Description: This portion of the Bitterroot Range is heavily dissected with massive forested ridges and clumps of summits just above timberline. Elevation span 5600'— the mountains aren't that high, but the valleys are really deep.

Geology: Sedimentary rocks uplifted and the upper layers departed eastward and now rest in the Missions, Swans and the Bob Marshall. The edge of the Idaho Batholith, just west of Lolo Hot Springs, accounts for granitic rocks.

Access: West of Missoula. Forest roads from Highway 200 and Interstate 90 reach the high country, including some summits. Trails approach most other peaks.

Ownership: Lolo and Coeur d'Alene national forests.

NORTH OF INTERSTATE 90

Gem Peak 6092 [D] Manned lookout.

Eighty Peak 6470 [P] Old radio facility and lookout site. The road is barely suitable for cars.

Bottle Peak 6305 [W] A short, obvious scramble up the east side from a trail.

Eightysevenmile Peak 5617 [W]

Minton Peak 5351 [J] Lookout tower.

Lost Peak 5930 [S] South ridge.

Bloom Peak 5863 [W] Old lookout site.

Black Peak 6548 [W] Old lookout site.

Sex Peak 5798 [W] Short walk from a car road. Lookout cabin built 1948. Peak named when two naked lovers were spotted here from a low-flying plane.

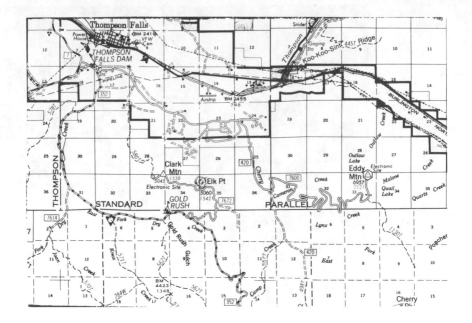

Clear Peak 6660 [W] Short walk from P-rated road.

Driveway Peak 6407 [D] Old lookout cabin.

Burke Summit 6580 [S] North approach from Burke Summit Pass.

Taft Summit 6296 [D] Old lookout site.

Mt. Bushnell 5980 [D] Old lookout site.

■ **Eddy Mountain 6957** [D] A mile west of Thompson Falls, on the west side of the Clark Fork River Bridge, turn south off Highway 200 onto the Prospect Creek Road. Within two miles, take two left turns to the Cherry Creek Road. In about nine miles take the Eddy Mountain Road. You'll climb 4000' in ten miles and find a lookout building (built 1982), a 4500' drop northeast to the Clark Fork River, and a nice view.

Cherry Peak 7360 [S] Approach on a trail from the north. The last 1½ miles is a bushwhack through scrubby timber to ascend an easy grassy ridge. The timbered summit has a small meadow on top.

Penrose Peak 7231 [W] Old lookout site.

Camels Hump 5888 [D] Manned lookout.

Patrick's Knob 6837 [D] Manned lookout. Radio facilities.

Keystone Peak 5878 [D] Old lookout site.

Siegel Mountain 6603 [W] Old lookout site.

Three Lakes Peak 7792 [W] Short scramble from trail to actual summit. North summit is highest.

Blackrock Peak 7628 [S] West ridge from trail.

Warden Mountain 7067 [S] West ridge. Peak on Flathead Indian Reservation.

Looking southeast from Eighty Peak. Bottle Peak near right margin

Gem Peak Lookout

It's a grassy stroll to the summit of Cherry Peak.

4500' from the Clark Fork River to the top of Eddy Mountain, center, rated D

■ **Squaw Peak 7996** [S] Leave Interstate 90 23 miles west of Missoula (at Exit 82) and head north three miles to the Ninemile Ranger Station. Use the map below to follow Road No. 2178, which ends in the middle of Section 21. From there walk up the trail 2½ miles, then scramble up the west ridge of the mountain. A little longer approach is from Edith Pass, the advantage being that Road No. 476 is a better road. Also, you'll probably want to leave the trail early to scramble up the southeast ridge.

Stark Mountain 7349 [D] Manned lookout. In recent summers the premises have been patrolled by cats, which means a little cheese will make friends in high places.

Alberton Beacon 5873 [J]

SOUTH OF INTERSTATE 90

Quarles Peak 6560 [J] Lookout site in Idaho, on south end of the summit.

Up Up Mountain 5969 [D] Manned lookout.

Gold Peak 7088 [W] Old lookout site.

Eagle Peak 7333 [W]

Ward Peak 7312 [W] Old lookout site.

Little Joe Mountain 7052 [W] Old lookout site.

Eagle Cliff 7543 [W]

Binocular Peak 7266 [W]

Illinois Peak 7690 [W] Old lookout site. Broad grassy summit, with exceptional views of Idaho backcountry.

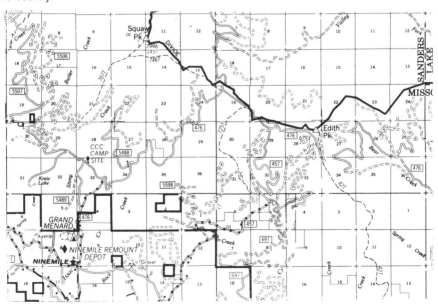

Squaw Peak from the southeast. Three Lakes Peak on right skyline

East side of Stark Mountain

Landowner Mountain 6985 [W] Old lookout.

Quartz Point 7770 [S] North or south ridge from trail.

Lightning Peak 7440 [W]

Saint Patrick Peak 7124 [W] Old lookout site.

Williams Peak 5640 [D] Manned lookout.

Crater Mountain 7663 [S] Climb the south spur of the east ridge and follow the ridge on up, or leave trail on the west side where it crosses the state line and follow the west ridge around.

Straight Peak 7646 [S] Short scramble up the south ridge from trail.

Admiral Peak 7323 [W]

Schley Mountain 7324 [W] Pronounced sha-lay. Drive car to pass just north of the summit, then hike up old jeep trail.

White Mountain 6524 [P] Lookout tower.

Shale Mountain 7612 [S] Depending on route chosen, some C-rated climbing may be necessary. Taller peak to the south is 7980' Rhodes Peak in Idaho.

Granite Peak 7551 [S] North ridge from trail.

Pilot Knob 7262 [W]

Deer Peak 6719 [P] Old lookout site. Cars easily get to within ½ mile of summit, maybe closer.

Martin Peak 6034 [P]

Petty Mountain 7270 [W] Old lookout site. High point of grassy ridgetop over five miles long.

Wild Horse Point 5805 [W] Old lookout site. Grassy ridgetop.

Telephone Butte 6885 [P] Old lookout site.

Blue Mountain 6460 [D] Manned lookout.

Eagle Peak from the southeast, with Square Lake, lower right

Crater Mountain from the southeast

Summit of Schley Mountain under autumn snow

Upper Cache Creek, from Schley Mountain to the north

White Mountain from the northwest

Pebble Creek, with Granite Peak on right center skyline. Note spires just under left center skyline.

Technical Opportunities: Practice areas include some rock outcrops near Harpers Bridge west of Missoula, and an assortment of granitic boulders and spires strewn through the woods in and just west of Lolo Hot Springs. For project climbs, bad rock enthusiasts head for Devils Gap up Marten Crook west of Noxon Reservoir. Those who prefer solid granite try Cache and Pebble creeks. There are spires in Pebble Creek, and a large tooth-shaped outcrop in Cache Creek which will someday undoubtedly have a route named Cache 22. Up on the stateline divide are leaning outcrops. Ice climbers can take a look from Highway 200 at the south side of the Clark Fork River about 10 miles east of Thompson Falls. If it's winter, you'll see a 400' icicle.

Bad rock and good rock: Devils Gap (left) and the Cache Creek tooth (right)

Krinklehorn Peak from the northwest

Wolverine Lakes from the east. Green Mountain (left) and Poorman Mountain (right) overlook the lake.

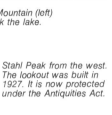

Stahl Peak from the west. The lookout was built in 1927. It is now protected under the Antiquities Act.

The Whitefish Range

"Both man and mountains have emerged from the same original earth and therefore have something in common between them."

—Sir Francis Younghusband

Description: A compact uniform range with a 5500' elevation span. Heavily forested slopes, ridgetop trails and open grassy summits.

Geology: Bands of billion-year-old limestone and shale slid eastward from the Purcell Mountains area and were glaciated here. This Whitefish Block didn't slide as far as the strata in Glacier National Park, and consequently didn't jumble as much.

Access: North of Kalispell. Forest highways from Highway 93 branch out into a network of logging roads, with trails to subalpine areas.

Ownership: Kootenai and Flathead national forests.

Poorman Mountain 7832 [W] Old lookout site.

Green Mountain 7830 [W]

Ksanka Peak 7505 [S] Northeast ridge.

Saint Clair Peak 7267 [S] Northwest ramp. East side cliffy.

Stahl Peak 7435 [W] Old cupola-design lookout.

Mt. Wam 7210 [W] Lookout cabin built 1931.

Tuchuck Mountain 7751 [W] Old lookout site. Completely deforested by fire.

Mt. Hefty 7585 [W] Old lookout cabin. High point of a ridge that runs into Canada.

Thoma Point 7180 [W] High point of a long ridge. Old lookout cabin.

Cleft Rock Mountain 7300 [W]

Mt. Thompson-Seton 7825 [W] Old lookout site.

Hornet Mountain 6744 [W] Short hike to old lookout building.

Krag Peak 7510 [S] South ridge.

Krinklehorn Peak 7411 [S] South ridge. Broken cliffs on east and north sides.

Deep Mountain 7406 [W]

Mt. Petery 7350 [S] North ridge. Forest Service map shows this peak a mile west of its actual location in Section 18.

Tuchuck Mountain's southwest side   South side of Nasukoin Mountain

■ **Mt. Marston 7343** [D] Turn east off Highway 93 ½ mile north of Stryker onto the Stillwater River Road No. 900. In about nine miles take a left onto the Mt. Marston Road and follow it about seven miles. Maintained lookout building on top.

Mt. Locke 7205 [W] Locke Point, on trail 1½ miles south of this summit, has a lookout cabin built in 1929.

Nasukoin Mountain 8095 [W] Stands of alpine larch line trail. Remains of old map tables are on both east and west summits.

Lake Mountain 7814 [W]

Cyclone Peak 6031 [W] Maintained lookout tower. Good views of Glacier National Park.

Stryker Peak 7338 [W] East face. Drive to 6900' to radio facilities and lookout building on Stryker Ridge.

Diamond Peak 7305 [W] Point 7445 is on ridgetop trail one mile north.

Moose Peak 7531 [W] Old lookout site.

Werner Peak 6960 [D] Maintained lookout building.

Big Mountain 6817 [J] Ski lift to top.

Lion Mountain 4387 [S] Southeast ridge from Highway 93. This solitary mound 1½ miles west of Whitefish actually looks like a lion.

Teakettle Mountain 5936 [J] East approach. Radio facilities on top. West side defoliated by air pollution from the aluminum plant at its base, which has since cleaned up its emissions.

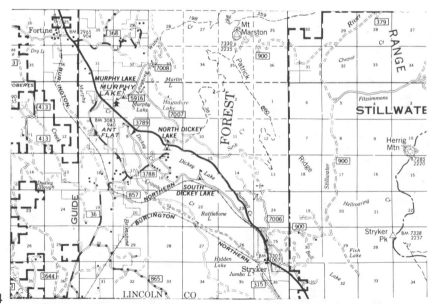

Diamond Peak Ridge from the north

Moose Peak from the east

Lookout buildings: Clockwise from top left—Stahl Peak, Mt. Wam, Cyclone Peak, and Hornet Mountain. It is illegal to vandalize any of these structures. They are monuments to man's solitary presence in these mountains.

Technical Opportunities: Exposed rock is available in the Krag and Stahl peaks areas. Quality climbing is limited due to the loose and crumbly nature of the rock and rolling nature of the range.

The Chief Mountain Highway. Mt. Cleveland's huge east face is on the center skyline. Stoney Indian Peaks are on the left skyline. U.S. Forest Service

Glacier National Park

"The lonely sunsets flame and die;
  The giant valleys gulp the night;
The monster mountains scrape the sky,
  Where eager stars are diamond-bright."

—Robert Service

Description: A massive compact jumble of completely glaciated sedimentary strata—broken cliffs and walls, long slopes of loose rock. Lower slopes heavily forested and often brushy. Elevation span of 7200' is so abrupt that the range generates its own weather.

Geology: The most spectacular portion of the Overthrust Belt—blocks of limestone and argillite (hard shale) up to a billion years old and thousands of feet thick skidded in from the west to rest on rock only 70 million years old. The journey resulted in great jumbling of the layers. Glaciers then sculpted the precise wild forms now here for your amusement.

Access: Northeast of Kalispell. A complete trail system comes in from all perimeter roads. Going-to-the-Sun Highway provides easy approaches to the central peaks.

Background: Glacier National Park is managed for a delicate balance wherein the raw beauty and wilderness atmosphere of the place can be experienced by hordes of people. In other words, a few regulations are necessary so that the Park Service can preserve the area. The two rules of most importance to climbers are: 1. You cannot go into areas closed because of bear danger, and 2. You need a camping permit to use any campground, or a backcountry permit in areas where campsites aren't designated. Concerning bears, there are hundreds of black and grizzly bears in the park. As long as people are occasionally mauled by them, and killed in their tents, you can expect the rangers to prosecute anyone going into closed areas. As for camping permits, the rangers check those, too. (If a camping permit is that much of a hassle, you probably shouldn't be climbing in the park anyway, since the peaks require patience and rational decision-making.) When you do get your permit and head out, take a cook stove, since wood fires aren't permitted.

Once you have accommodated the wildland bureaucracy, you'll hopefully appreciate that the Park Service is there to help you. You should register with the rangers before climbing. Though not required, it is appreciated, and is for your own good. Be sure to check in on your way out, too. You can also stop in at any Subdistrict office for updated information on trails and campgrounds, and sometimes even the condition of the climbing route you are contemplating. If you have doubts about information, talk to one of the rangers. Seasonal employees are not always a reliable source of information. Most accident victims are not visitors but seasonal employees who disregard the warnings.

Kintla Peak from the northeast, with remaining early summer snow

Southeast face of Mt. Peabody

Now you know that to do a major peak in Glacier National Park you must have plenty of time, bear clearance, a camping permit, and a good weather forecast. Also, if you've never climbed in the park, try a small peak first to get used to the rock, and also to understand how the climbs are rated. Once on your way, you need to be especially cautious about wet rock. Waterfall areas are particularly dangerous. The rock is such that, when wet, it is perfectly slippery, and every year more tragedies are instigated by wet rock than by any other hazard. Another very real danger is the crevasses in the glaciers. Do not travel on glaciers unless they are on your intentional route and you know how to deal with them. That goes for steep snowfields, too. Solo climbs involving glacier travel shouldn't be considered.

Still interested in the great mountains of Glacier National Park? Then you owe it to yourself to pick up a copy of J. Gordon Edwards's *A Climber's Guide to Glacier National Park*. It is an excellent book and very detailed. If you don't care for detailed route descriptions and prefer to repeat the mistakes others have made, you could still use a copy for the valuable background information it provides. You can use Edwards's route descriptions in conjunction with the photographs found in this chapter, as many of them were specifically included for such a comparison. Some experienced climbers consider some of the moves Edwards mentions around *route obstacles* to be overstated. While this may sometimes be true, never consider any of the *hazards* he mentions to be similarly overstated. His time allowances aren't exaggerated, either.

One last note: In this chapter, the presence of a register isn't noted in the peak descriptions. Just about every major peak and pinnacle in the park has one, usually in a compact shale cairn.

NORTH OF GOING-TO-THE-SUN ROAD
Livingstone Range

Long Knife Peak 9784 [C] Bushwhack to the east ramp. You may want to rope up on the summit pinnacles.

Parke Peak 9038 [S] Northwest cirque route. Old triangulation station on summit. One day climb if you use a boat on Kintla Lake.

Kinnerly Peak 9944 [C] Northwest face. The route is trying, the correct break through the high cliffs difficult to find. It's particularly hard to downclimb, so be sure to mark your route with ducks for the descent. May as well take a rope. The east face (T-rated) has also been climbed.

58   *Two looks at twin summits: Labyrinth summit of Kinnerly Peak (left) and summit pyramid of Kintla Peak*

Climbers must find a route up cliffs high on the northwest side of Kinnerly Peak.

Vulture Peak from the southeast

Kintla Peak 10101 [C] Northeast ridge, reached from Agassiz Creek and the trail above Upper Kintla Lake—an unusually scenic approach. A three-day trip.

Numa Point 6960 [W] Lookout, manned since 1934.

Numa Peak 9003 [C] Southeast face from Bowman Lake.

Mt. Peabody 9216 [S] Notheast ridge. A complex route, exposed on the ridgetop.

Boulder Peak 8528 [C] Easy trip up the northwest ridge from Boulder Pass.

Mt. Custer 8883 [C] Southwest ridge. Mostly a scramble, but a few spots are exposed.

Chapman Peak 9406 [S] From the southwest.

Thunderbird Mountain 8790 [S] West face from Brown Pass. The snow goes out late.

The Sentinel 8835 [S]

The Guardhouse 9336 [S]

Porcupine Ridge 9128 [C]

Rainbow Peak 9891 [S] West face from Bowman Lake. Mostly a scramble, but figure on a little C-rated climbing to avoid spending time on route-finding once you get about half way up. A longer alternative route is the southeast ridge.

Mt. Carter 9843 [S] Northwest couloir. You may encounter a touch of C-rated climbing. Time permitting, the ridge connecting Carter to Rainbow Peak is a nice S-rated route.

Vulture Peak 9638 [S] From Vulture Glacier. Plan for glacier travel. The climb can also be made up the southeast shoulder.

Nahsukin Mountain 8194 [S]

Mt. Geduhn 8414 [S] Take the north ridge to the central peak, then head southeast to the highest point.

Scorpion-shaped Mt. Custer from the south

Southwest side of Mt. Chapman

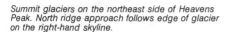

Summit glaciers on the northeast side of Heavens Peak. North ridge approach follows edge of glacier on the right-hand skyline.

Huckleberry Mountain Lookout overlooks Livingstone Range portion of the park. In the distance is Longfellow Peak. Paul Bunyan's Cabin visible on the south ridge.

Anaconda Peak 8279 [C]

Longfellow Peak 8904 [C] Northeast ridge, or from Dutch Lakes. Ice axes and a rope may be needed for protection on snowfields on the northeast ridge route. Paul Bunyan's Cabin, 8490', a black monolith high on Longfellow's narrow south ridge, is a T-rated climb.

Heavens Peak 8987 [C] North or south ridge. The north ridge is reached by the Glacier Wall, a ridge that extends eastward down through a burned area to McDonald Creek. Start from Logan Creek, Packers Roost, or the avalanche exhibit on the Going-to-the-Sun Road. Wherever you start, it's still a long day. Take an ice axe in early summer.

McPartland Mountain 8413 [S]

Mt. Vaught 8850 [C] Southwest ridge from Mt. Stanton.

Stanton Mountain 7750 [C] Southeast side. Only a small amount of C-rated climbing is necessary.

Huckleberry Mountain 6593 [W] Manned lookout.

Lewis Range—North of Swiftcurrent Creek

Miche Wabun Peak 8861 [C] Southeast face. You may want to use a rope.

Kaina Mountain 9489 [S] South ridge.

Mt. Cleveland 10466 [C] West or southwest face. A long grind up this monster. Obstacles of time, weather, and fatigue turn back 75% of the 200 or so climbers who attempt this peak each summer. The elk trails referred to by Edwards may be hard to find. You can get up-to-the-minute route information at the Goat Haunt Ranger Station. They also have aerial photos you can study. Normally, you'll want to leave the trail before you get to Kootenai Lakes. On the west face route, above the falls, you get to do a lot of route-finding on the steep 3000' slope. There's a real tendency here to kick rocks down onto your partners. The southwest face route is a little easier, with so few broken cliffs that it almost rates an S. The loose scree, however, is endless, and getting to that face takes a little longer. If you're already in the backcountry, the ridge connecting Stoney Indian Peaks with Cleveland is nice. You start at Stoney Indian Lake (Note: trail to timberline!), do a high traverse (rated C) on the east side of Stoney Indian Peak, then scramble up the spacious south ridge of Cleveland. This ridge can also be reached from Whitecrow Lake.

And then there's this thing called the north face, the greatest sudden piece of vertical topography in the lower 48 states. Edwards's description: "It is NOT really a high, sheer cliff, as it appears from below. Instead it is a great complicated rock mountainside, slanting at perhaps 60 degrees as it

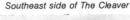

North face of Mt. Cleveland —Kalispell Weekly News

Southeast side of The Cleaver

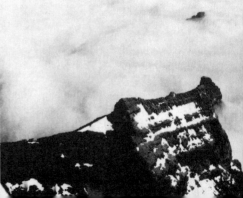

Chief Mountain looks east across the Montana prairie.

rises nearly 4000 vertical feet." (And that's starting 2000' above Waterton Lake.) "That mountainside is a chaotic jumble of pinnacles, couloirs, chimneys, ledges, and ridges, with a few impressive cliffs interspersed. The ridges and pinnacles often stand apart from the main face by a distance of 40' to 100', and easy routes may lie hidden behind those visible structures." There's also a great scree ledge cutting across the face at 9000', accessible from the west face. It does of course carry snow late into the summer. Anyway, the face has been climbed, and it rates a good solid T. The east side of Cleveland is also technical, with rugged icefalls in the Whitecrow Glacier and falling rock in the great runnels on the face.

Point 9996 (The Cleaver) [C] Southeast ramp. Mostly scrambling, but a little C-rated ground near the top. This is the hatchet-shaped peak on Cleveland's northeast ridge.

Stoney Indian Peak 9350 [C]

Chief Mountain 9080 [S] West slope, generally reached by coming around the south side of the mountain from the east. A direct approach from the east on the high prairie will avoid horrible aspen thickets. If you come in on the jeep trail, look a mile east of the peak for a stream channel which has been enlarged by flash run-offs from an old burn.

The east face is rated hard C and involves careful route finding. A T-rated route on the northeast face has been accomplished. Note: Chief is limestone and rotten even by park standards.

Cathedral Peak 9041 [C] Southwest approach.

Mt. Kipp 8839 [S] Southwest approach from nearby trail.

Mt. Merritt 10004 [C] North side approach, gained from Mokowanis Lake. When in the valley just below Margaret Lake and just south of the heavy timber, find two gullies low on the west side of Merritt. Climb on elk trails between the gullies, taking the north gully if you lose the trail. Just below the cliffs the trail levels off and contours around the mountain into the north cirque. In the cirque, climb to the highest point of the talus slope. Three couloirs are there. Take the one on the right,

*t. Merritt from the southeast. (Note: Summit of
*Merritt, with Nacoas Peak below, pictured on the title
age.)
　　　　　　　　　—Cal Tassinari

Southwest slopes of Mt. Gould

Southwest side of Mt. Siyeh

starting on the west (right) side of it to clear some small cliffs and continue up to the saddle. Above there, Old Sun Glacier has receded and you shouldn't have to venture out on it. Merritt has two summits, within two or three feet of being the same height. The north one, straight up the ridge from the saddle, has the register. When the weather is good, there is no finer view in all of Montana than the view from the summit of Merritt. If you're really lucky, you'll see and hear the ice fall off the snout of Old Sun Glacier. A route up this glacier is seldom done. This interesting southeast approach requires endurance and technical skill with ice axes, rope, and crampons.

Natoas Peak 9476 [C] Scramble in from the saddle to the north, on the Mt. Merritt route. The top is less than a yard wide, and it's a 1000' drop on two sides.

Ipasha Peak 9572 [S] South approach from Ahern Peak. T-rated on the northeast arete.

Ahern Peak 8749 [W] Goat trail up the southeast ridge.

Gable Mountain 9262 [S] South or east ridge.

Seward Mountain 8917 [S] Southwest ridge from Redgap Pass.

Crowfeet Mountain 8914 [S] North ridge (attained from the west), or from Mt. Henkel.

Mt. Henkel 8770 [S] South couloir.

Altyn Peak 7947 [S] Climb from saddle west of peak. Attain saddle from the south.

Appekunny Mountain 9068 [S] Attain east ridge from the south.

Iceberg Peak 9146 [S] Can be done from Iceberg Notch. The route up to the notch is a little difficult to follow. The goat trails have multiplied and often dead-end. The route is blind when downclimbing. Otherwise, the notch route is also S-rated.

There's a T-rated climb on a feature called B7 Pillar near the notch. The route goes up a chimney on the north side.

Mt. Gould—the symbol of Glacier National Park—from the east

Mt. Wilbur 9321 [T] East face. This climb has been done without protection, but exposure is encountered near the top, and experienced climbers should at least take a sling or short rope to tie in and rest. Also, early summer snow is so steep that protection is required then. Naturally, a mountain like Wilbur has many variants. A difficult route on the north face from Iceberg Lake goes something like this: When about 300' below the diorite sill (a dark band of igneous rock), enter a damp slippery chimney. Once above the diorite, the chimney overhangs and is interspersed with large chockstones. Then the chimney widens into a chute, and an exposed face remains before a final scramble to the summit.

Lewis Range—South of Swiftcurrent Creek

Swiftcurrent Mountain 8436 [W] Manned lookout.

Mt. Grinnell 8851 [S]

Mt. Gould 9553 [S] Southwest side from trail. Mostly a long steep scramble. The mighty east face rates a capital T.

Allen Mountain 9376 [S] South slope from Cracker Lake. There are several harder but more interesting routes from the north.

Wynn Mountain 8404 [S] South ridge, gained from the west.

Pollock Mountain 9190 [S] At the first stream east of Logan Pass, take a faint trail, staying east of the stream to get past some cliffs. From the top of the southeast ridge use a couloir through cliffs under the summit on the east side, or an interesting cleft on the south side.

Piegan Mountain 9220 [S]

■ **Mt. Siyeh 10014** [S] Easiest of the six 10000' peaks in the park, and done in a day if you're in good shape. Park at Siyeh Bend, on the Going-to-the-Sun Road three miles east of Logan Pass, and take the Cut-off trail for a little over a mile, then hang a left onto the Piegan Pass-Siyeh Pass Trail. Walk another 1½ miles and you'll be at another trail junction near timberline. Go right, up toward Siyeh Pass about ¼ mile and study the broad south slope of Siyeh, which has some vegetated strips starting up it. Take the one on the right, then work on up a stream bed to clear a line of cliffs, always angling right if you encounter a problem. After this short C-rated pitch, it's just a long scramble to the top. From the Piegan Pass trail it is possible to find an S-rated break through the line of cliffs on the west ridge of the mountain, then scramble up the edge of the north face drop off. The northeast ridge route from Wynn Mountain has a similar finish. Is the north face a T-rated route? Don't ask. This book rates climbing routes, not air shows. Edwards's book has two photos of J. Gordon himself having lunch on the lip of that 3000' vertical drop. It appears this mountain wasn't eroded but that half was sawed off and taken away.

A sea of clouds laps at the halfway mark on the 3000' north wall of Mt. Siyeh.

63

Going-to-the-Sun Mountain from the west

Walking south up the summit ridge of Going-to-the-Sun Mountain

Mataphi Peak 9365 [S] East face is a T-rated climb.

Going-to-the-Sun Mountain 9642 [C] West face, with the diagonal snow chute as an option. Mostly a scramble, but some careful C-rated climbing is required on any route. The east face south of Sexton Glacier is a C-rated route, but the route-finding is more tedious. Also, you'll need ice axe and crampons to go up a snowfield. It's not real steep, but the run-out is bad (broken and rocky). Between the glacier and the snow you'll be dealing with a little exposure. Other approaches include the southeast shoulder or buttress, and the southwest ridge. The south face is progressively more technical as you go up. Be set to rappell off if you can't complete the route.

Goat Mountain 8826 [S] From Baring Creek.

East Flattop Mountain 8356 [S]

SOUTH OF GOING-TO-THE-SUN ROAD

Logan Pass Area

■ **Mt. Oberlin 8180** [S] Park at the visitors' center at Logan Pass on the Going-to-the-Sun Road. Now inspect the southeast slope of Oberlin to determine a route free of cliffs and snowfields, then head up, only 1500' vertical. There's a smidgeon of C-rated climbing on the summit knob. The complete round trip, including an hour on top, shouldn't take over four hours. This is the easiest major peak in the park, and a perfect introduction to climbing there.

Mt. Cannon 8952 [C] East ridge from Hidden Pass. Route somewhat complex, and rock rotten, but mostly a scramble. Edwards suggests going right (north) of the southeast shoulder. Some climbers go straight up on the shoulder.

Clements Mountain 8760 [S] West ridge from Hidden Pass. On the ridge there is a narrow trail traverse with thrilling exposure. Other approaches on Clements are more difficult. The east side is a C-rated climb if the correct route is found.

Northeast side of Mt. Oberlin

Happy climbers on Oberlin's summit
—Kalispell Weekly News

Clements Mountain from the south

North side of Reynolds Mountain. Note the diagonal ledge high on the face.

Bearhat Mountain 8684 [S] A difficult scramble, perhaps with some C-rated moves to avoid wandering all over the side of the mountain. Climb the east face to the left of the great rift.

Reynolds Mountain 9125 [C] Southwest side. An interesting variant of the southwest route is to climb up the dominant large cleft, on the right-hand side (east end) of the peak, which begins at the top of the extensive talus slope. Just about where this cleft turns into a tight chimney, find a ledge to the left (west) and follow it across the southwest face to where it fades out. In this vicinity locate a way to a higher ledge. A little more careful route-finding will have you on top. Another C-rated route is the east couloir, reached using the diagonal ledge which crosses the north face. This exciting route is a little harder than the southwest approach, especially for downclimbing, and it calls for a little more judgment and ability to appreciate blind exposure. If conditions are good and the snow has melted off the diagonal ledge, the route can be done without a rope. If conditions are not good, the route is strictly a technical effort. A direct ascent of the north face is of course a T-rated climb. A route has been done there to the dip in the middle of the summit crown.

Mt. Brown Lookout 7487 [W]
Mt. Brown 8565 [C] Southwest ridge.
Little Matterhorn 7886 [C] Southeast face.
Edwards Mountain 9072 [S] East face.
Gunsight Mountain 9258 [S] West face snowfield from the Sperry Headwall Stairway. Ice axes recommended. West peak is the highest.

East face of Bearhat Mountain, showing the great rift

Business end of Mt. Cannon (west side) —Kalispell Weekly News

Coming and going on the diagonal ledge on Mt. Reynolds

Mt. Jackson 10052 [S] Northeast ridge, from the northwest or east. Use the northwest option (Edwards's Route B) for the ascent, as it has better rock holds and less off-trail elevation. For the descent, the east option (Edwards's Route A) provides better scree running slopes. On the extreme northwest side of the peak are 60 degree ice gullies and a steep glacier, all suitable for ice technicians.

Walton Mountain 8926 [T] John-boy never sailed up this one. You need, as a minimum, ropes and ice axes to get to the ridge between Jackson and Walton. Once off the ice, it's a testy scramble on better-than-average rock. Follow the north ridge to the base of the peak, then swing out onto the west side to find gullies and chimmeys to alternate with the ridge until the top is reached.

Blackfoot Mountain 9574 [T] North side. Rope and ice axe required for technical ice protection. Crampons recommended.

Mt. Logan 9239 [S]

Citadel Mountain 9030 [C] West approach to the south ridge.

Almost-a-Dog Mountain 8922 [S]

Little Chief Mountain 9541 [S] West side. Edwards suggests ascending a broad talus gully (an avalanche chute), or try an ascending traverse, angling right (to the south). A T-rated route has been done, directly up the cirque, up the entire northeast face. The lower half was reported to be "real steep."

Mahtotopa Mountain 8672 [S]

Red Eagle Mountain 8881 [S]

66   *Mt. Jackson's northeast side, showing the ridge used for most ascents*   *North side of Gunsight Mountain, and Sperry Glacier*

Walton Mountain from the south. Harrison Glacier is east (right) of the north ridge, which connects Walton to Mt. Jackson.

North side of Blackfoot Mountain, and Blackfoot Glacier

Two Medicine Area

Split Mountain 8792 [T] Southeast approach. Exposed rock work at the top.
Norris Mountain 8882 [S] Southeast ridge from Triple Divide Peak.
Triple Divide Peak 8020 [S] Short scramble from Triple Divide Pass. Water from this mountain goes to the Pacific Ocean, the Gulf of Mexico, and Hudson's Bay.
Mt. James 9375 [S] West ridge from Triple Divide Pass.
Kupunkamint Mountain 8797 [S]
Red Mountain 9377 [S]
Flinsch Peak 9225 [S] South ridge from Dawson Pass. Easy scramble from trail in the pass.
Rising Wolf Mountain 9513 [S] West ridge. Man and goat trails most of the way. A long scree scramble can also be made up a ramp on the south side of the east ridge, starting at a gully near the inlet of Two Medicine Lake. You can see the Two Medicine Chalet from the top. Climbers sometimes try to shortcut to the lake down the southeast side of the mountain, only to be stranded by cliffs when tired and running out of daylight. Fatalities in the cliffs have resulted. Allow plenty of time. If you don't, still go down a route you know.
Sinopah Mountain 8271 [S]
Mt. Rockwell 9272 [C] West face, reached from above Cobalt Lake. Exceptional view.
Grizzly Mountain 9067 [S]
Mt. Henry 8847 [S] Northeast ridge.

Nyack Wilderness Zone

In this area access is often via a ford of the Middle Fork of the Flathead River. The ford is a major undertaking. A boat is often necessary. Also, the channels and creeks change every year. Contact Walton Ranger Station for current information.

Loneman Mountain 7181 [W] Manned lookout.
Mt. Thompson 8527 [S]
Threesuns Mountain 8205 [C]

West side of Little Chief Mountain   Mt. James from the east   67

Downclimbing a steep gully in the park

Mad Wolf Mountain from the southeast. One of several flat-topped mountains on the east side of the park, not listed as peaks, making for nice high-elevation strolls in wind, flowers, and scenery

Mt. Stimson 10142 [C] Not for sleek, pampered climbers. Only wilderness animals need show up. The northwest face route is a three-day trip, and there is some exposure. Often the route is cold and icy, with no sunshine till late in the day. About five parties a year now attempt this colossus. There were some years in the 1970s when no one made the summit. To start up the mountain from Nyack Creek, you might veer to the left (northeast) of the stream mentioned by Edwards so as to climb through a Douglas-fir stand instead of endless downfalls. Once in that open timber stand, angle to the right as you climb until just below some cliffs, then return to the stream and climb in the channel or through diminishing brush. The large waterfall at about 6500' can be climbed on either side, and is probably easiest five to ten feet to the right side. From the top of the waterfall do as Edwards suggests: Head directly to the summit. If you make a small traverse to find a break in the endless lines of cliffs, a returning traverse the same distance should be made above the difficult pitch. Set plenty of ducks to guide you back down. You don't have time to get lost. Once above the saddle, the yellow rock traverse comes out just above a large rock hump on the southwest ridge. The ridge itself is not difficult.

There may be easier routes waiting to be tried. The cirque south of the southwest ridge would be a likely choice, if an elk trail up Pinchot Creek could be located. The southwest ridge itself appears to be a spectacular C-rated climb. One could start on the southeast side of Nyack Creek by heading up a scree draw which hits the ridge just left of a low point just left (northeast) of Threesuns Mountain.

Mt. Pinchot 9310 [S] South face from Buffalo Woman Lake.

Eaglehead Mountain 9140 [S]

Mt. Phillips 9494 [S]

Peril Peak 8645 [S]

The summit and east ridge of Rising Wolf Mountain

Flinsch Peak from Rising Wolf Mountain. Dawson Pass, left

View from the south of Mt. Stimson, the most physically demanding climb in the park

Mt. Doody 8800 [S]
Battlement Mountain 8830 [S]
Vigil Peak 8593 [S]
Mt. Saint Nicholas 9376 [T] This peak is famous as the most technically demanding one in Glacier National Park. Actually, the technical climbing is pretty straightforward on somewhat solid rock. The bushwhack in, however, is the stuff legends are made of. First of all, no fair crossing the Middle Fork of the Flathead at the mouth of Park Creek—it's private land. Use the highway bridge instead and park at the Walton Range Station. Stop in for the latest conditions. Then head out on the trail and up Park Creek. The idea is to climb up to a saddle just northeast of Salvage Mountain and then follow the ridge around and locate a game trail down to the lake at the base of Saint Nick's east side. To get from Park Creek to the saddle, look for a gully southwest of the creek that drains from it, about two miles past the Muir Creek trail junction. This route will save you dealing with some brush. An upper fork of Muir Creek goes directly to the base of Saint Nick from a trail, but this is a brushy affair, not a good ascent route. (However, as brush grows downhill, you can go with the grain when you leave.) Once at the lake on Saint Nick's east side, head up to the great notch on the northeast ridge, where the technical climbing begins. About five parties a year make this climb. Different strategies have been used above the notch, but the best one appears to be to go straight up the ridge without zig-zagging. Friends (the mechanical devices) work well for protection. When rappelling on the descent be careful with the rope as it is easy to get hung up in cracks. More difficult routes have been accomplished. The southwest face is perhaps the most appealing chance on the mountain. The north side of the west ridge is particularly interesting as it has several ways where one could *almost* walk right up to the top, with an apparent obstacle at the end of each way.

Southwest face of notorious Mt. Saint Nicholas.

Mt. Saint Nicholas from the east, with the great notch on the right —Jim Ullrich

69

Church Butte 8808 [S]
Salvage Mountain 8328 [S]
Mt. Despair 8582 [C]
Point 8888 [S] This point is just southwest of Mt. Despair, west of Lost Basin.
Brave Dog Mountain 8446 [S]
Sheep Mountain 8569 [S]
Scalplock Mountain 6919 [W] Old lookout site. A good family hike.
Running Rabbit Mountain 7674 [S]
Elk Mountain 7835 [S] Old lookout site. You may still be able to locate the trail.
Little Dog Mountain 8610 [S]
Summit Mountain 8770 [S]

Technical Opportunities: Significant technical routes up the major peaks have been mentioned. In addition, there are many smaller formations, such as the Garden Wall Spires, and Citadel Spire on Porcupine Ridge. No direct aid is necessary to climb the major technical peaks of the park by the easiest route, but direct aid is often necessary on the more difficult routes and vertical walls.

There's a good practice area outside Avalanche Campground, between Logan and Avalanche creeks, at the base of Mt. Cannon. Using the crack systems in those vertical, broken cliffs it is possible to put up a five- to six-pitch climb. Also, winter brings many ice climbing opportunities. Birdwoman Falls, the Moose Country Exhibit area in McDonald Creek, and Nyack Creek are good places on the west side. These areas melt out early. There are also many waterfalls on the east side where the climate is drier and colder.

The main thing to remember about Glacier National Park is that all the technical climbing has not made the rock any better. Those who do well on the endless opportunities of shale and limestone are those who are used to the rock and have extensive experience on it. An example of local experience would be the use of protection which does not work an entire chunk of the attached face loose, desperately compounding whatever problem you might be having.

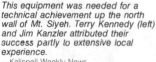

This equipment was needed for a technical achievement up the north wall of Mt. Siyeh. Terry Kennedy (left) and Jim Kanzler attributed their success partly to extensive local experience.
—Kalispell Weekly News

A young climber contemplates the east side of Mt. Gould from Piegan Pass. Years of experience, often from childhood, back those who succeed on such faces.
—Kalispell Weekly News

Climbers enjoy a rest high above Gray Wolf Lake —Cal Tassinari

The Mission Range

"We began the long hike out. This time we headed for the ridge trail, which although longer, is easier on tired feet going out. It was dark when we came to the road. We could see the full moon where at that very moment, men were walking on its surface."
—Rick Graetz, coming off McDonald Peak,
July 20, 1969.

Description: A very abrupt group of peaks. Nearly all of the 7000' elevation gain must be overcome on foot. The southern portion is heavily glaciated, has few trails, and tapers northward into a featureless flat ridge.

Geology: The shale strata in the Missions, part of the Overthrust Belt, is higher on the western side and slopes east. Consequently, routes are short and steep from the west, long and gentle from the east. Glacial remnants are still active up high. A recent continental ice sheet rode up over the northern end of the range to a point roughly east of Polson, grinding off peaks and leaving a long rounded dome without prominent features.

Access: East of Ronan. Branch roads from Highways 83 (east side) and 93 (west side) end at trailheads. The higher reaches are served only by trails and cross country routes.

Ownership: Flathead and Lolo national forests, Flathead Indian Reservation.

Background: The western half of this area is managed as Tribal Wilderness by the Flathead Indian Reservation. Tribal land is private and, not being subject to the usual federal laws, can be closed any time. Closures are enforced. Violators are prosecuted. Contact the tribe in Ronan for an information update if you're planning a trip. You'll need a Tribal Recreation Permit for any activities in the Tribal Wilderness. These can be obtained from retailers on the reservation, and also in nearby communities including Condon, Seeley Lake, and Missoula.

As a private wilderness area, the western Missions are managed more for the qualities they contain than for readily available wilderness experiences. Members of the tribe account for only five percent of the users, so it appears keeping the area as it was

View of Goat Peak from the west

The entire west face of Peak 8429 is a series of palisades.

before the white men came reflects respect for the land that is both a heritage and priority of the Flathead Tribe. Unlike federal wilderness, you may not be permitted to go in where and when you want. But when you can go, you will have a better opportunity for a first class wilderness experience. The most common reason for a wilderness closure is grizzly bear activity. Grizzlies range from Hellroaring Creek south to the Jocko River, and are concentrated around McDonald Peak. Since the tribe manages the area to prevent bear harassment by humans, with protection of humans being a secondary benefit, area closures can be expected as long as the grizzly is an endangered species.

Cedar Peak 7592 [S] Old lookout site. Southwest ridge.

Goat Peak 7995 [S] Gain the south or east ridge from the southeast.

Peak 8429 [C] Northwest ridge, or the east side from Terrace Lake. This is the broad peak so dominant just east of Ronan. It is at the head of Lost Creek and does not appear on the Forest Service map.

Cold Peak 8522 [C] Brushy approach from the South Fork of Cold Creek. This mountain used to be called Squaw Teton Peaks, with the split between the twin summits called Gunsight Notch. This summit does not appear on the Forest Service map.

■ **Mt. Harding 9061** [C] The northern summit is highest of the three. The southern, easiest one is a good way to start climbing in the Missions. Leave Highway 93 about 5½ miles south of Ronan, turning east onto the first county road north of the Allentown Motel. Go east exactly four miles, cross the irrigation canal, and turn left (north). In about ⅛ mile another road takes off uphill to the right (east). If the gate is locked, start walking here. Otherwise, drive as far as you care to, then hike up the trail toward Eagle Pass. Once out of the timber and just under the pass, work northward up steep meadows to the southwest ridge, then on up to the south peak, 8881'. The last 15 feet or so has some easy C-rated moves. If approaching the southwest ridge from the east side of Eagle Pass, expect steep snow requiring protection. The other two peaks can be reached from the south

Northwest shoulder of Mt. Harding. The summit is gained by the gully just to the right of the notch at the north end of the summit ridge.

West side of Cold Peak. The east face is also split by the large cleft.

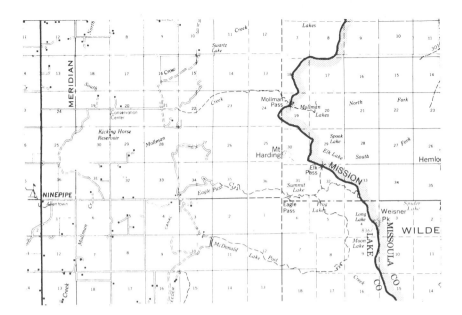

peak. A rope is necessary in early summer, as a snow bridge is usually present. The middle summit is ascended using a chimney on the east side. Working toward the north summit, the route alternates between the connecting ridge and the southeast face of the north peak. This entire traverse is rated C. T-rated routes are available from Summit Lake.

The most direct approach to the north summit is the northwest shoulder. Scramble up the shoulder till just under the top, traverse across the west face southward till about 50 yards past the notch, then take a steep gully, rated C, to the summit ridge and walk to the top. In early summer a cornice forms across the top and has proven fatal, so be careful. Also, if lightning is imminent or the rock becomes wet, you may want to rappel down the steep gully.

Weisner Peak 8367 [S] Register. South ridge approach. Named after a young lady with the Sierra Club, killed in an auto accident the day after climbing this peak.

Hemlock Point 7780 [W] Old lookout site. Hike the south ridge on an abandoned trail, or scramble up the southeast flank.

McDonald Peak 9820 [S] Register. Very early on a July morning as dawn warms this ancient peak and the snowfields take on a pink glow, grizzly bears begin to frolic in the freedom of summer. Damn big and nonchalant they stand, sniffing the air. They then lumber up the slopes to snack on ladybugs and army cutworm moths. After leisurely grubbing through rocks for these seasonal delicacies, the bears begin to overheat as the sun beats down on their thick fur. Since every summer day in the mountains is like a day off from work, the larger bears round up the cubs, and together amble up to the summit snowfields to cool off and have fun, lolling about in the drowsy afternoon hours, from time to time taking a whimsical glance at a good-sized chunk of the Western Hemisphere. As the pleasures of the day envelope them, these bears take on a sporting attitude, romping about on slush and loose shale until finally, overwhelmed by exuberance, they take off for the lower elevations, hurtling down steep snowfields at a full gallop, paws slashing out avalanches of slush while long claws serve as crampons. Once off the snow they disappear into lengthening

The three summits of Mt. Harding, from the southeast. Flathead Lake beyond in the Mission Valley —U.S. Forest Service

Placing the register on Weisner Peak —Cal Tassinari   **73**

shadows of evening at timberline. These patrols are repeated until September when insect food is no longer found, and the beasts head into the valleys.

This briefly explains why you can't just climb McDonald Peak anytime. As an area where grizzly bears are heavily concentrated, bear-human confrontations are not surprising. The Flathead Tribe now closes the entire area around the peak from July until after the bears have left sometime in September. Because this is a critical feeding area, you have to schedule your climb between the presence of bears and the first snows of winter, then hope for good weather. Actually, early autumn is probably the best time to climb this peak because of snow on the approaches earlier in the year.

There are several ways to the summit. The east approach is via Island Lake, which can be reached by a primitive trail from Heart Lake. Stay anywhere except Glacier Lake, which has been camped to shreds. From Island Lake head west on primitive trails to the top of the Mission Divide. Now gracefully surrender 800' of elevation to drop to Cliff Lake. (Don't worry about losing the elevation. You'll gain it right back on your way out!) Go directly for the outlet so as to head around the north side of the lake, selecting a route up the peak as you go. If you head up the east side snowfield you'll need an ice axe, although you can kick steps and shouldn't need crampons. A number of people have been hurt or killed after losing their footing on that snowfield and slipping to the rocks below. Sometimes late in the year you can find ways to avoid the snow, eliminating that hazard entirely. If you don't want to do the east side, head southwest from Cliff Lake around the south buttress of McDonald to the Ashley Creek Divide, then scramble up a long scree slope to the top of the buttress, and walk to the summit. Either way you go, it's a long day.

Looking toward Mt. Harding, center skyline, from Hemlock Point —Cal Tassinari

Northwest side of McDonald Peak, showing the route up the northwest glacier

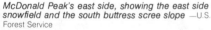

Looking west off McDonald Peak. Mission Valley 7000' below. Father Taleman and two friends made the first recorded climb in 1894. —Cal Tassinari

McDonald Peak's east side, showing the east side snowfield and the south buttress scree slope —U.S. Forest Service

74

Lake-of-the-Clouds on the north side of Glacier Peak. Daughter-of-the-Sun Mountain to the left —U.S. Forest Service

West side of Daughter-of-the-Sun Mountain —U.S. Forest Service

The northwest glacier route is also time consuming. It starts with a bushwhack from the upper end of McDonald Lake and is a brush ape's delight. Head south up the valley that runs into Sheephead Mountain, a peak on McDonald's west ridge. The next part of the route involves some technical brush scrambling up 70-degree slopes and avalanche debris to the left (east) of the long waterfall. Once in the cirque above the waterfall, you'll need a rope and ice axe for the glacier below the summit ridge. Crampons are recommended, as ice is often exposed. This route is not recommended in early summer due to falling cornices and avalanche danger.

A route completely free of avalanche danger (in the summer) is the bear-infested Ashley Creek approach. This area is not part of the summer grizzly phenomenon high on the peak. The grizzlies live in Ashley Creek year-round. A brushed-in trail will get you up it to Ashley Lakes. Above the second lake go up to the top of a prominent talus slope just north of the line of cliffs to find a goat trail that follows gullies and ledges on up through these cliffs. Above there head eastward for a couple of miles up the creek and scramble up steep loose shale to the summit. This is the most direct route, has no up-and-down, and is S-rated. On the other hand, you have to overcome 6400' of elevation on foot in a land where Grizzly is King. Going by Duncan Lake to get on the west ridge is a shorter option, but this route is a C-climb, with a rope recommended on the knifelike ridge. Footing is better, and you save the shale slopes for the descent. Or finally, you can do the entire west ridge, with considerable up-and-down. The more open timber and exposed ridge can minimize sudden bear confrontations. But remember, if you use any route in Ashley Creek, keep your party small and unobtrusive, as it is the desire of the Tribe that their great bears not be bothered.

Peak 8895 [S] North of Kakashe Peak. Not on the Forest Service map.

Kakashe Peak 8575 [S] From the east.

Glacier Peak 9402 [C] Northwest ridge. The west summit is the higher of this pair of peaks above Sunrise Glacier. Though basically a scramble, expect some exposure. Mt. Shoemaker is a prominent peak on the southeast ridge.

Panoramic Peak 8650 [S] Register. East side approach from Island Lake.

Mountaineer Peak 9261 [S] Register. The north face is a C-rated climb through sliding rock.

Daughter-of-the-Sun Mountain 8777 [C] Southeast ridge. The northeast ridge is brushy and requires some route-finding. The west ridge is begun from Turquoise Lake. Follow it on up, then traverse to a large draw on the south side of the mountain which goes up to the southeast ridge near the summit. Note: All routes eventually merge with the southeast ridge. Near the actual summit, thread through some house-sized blocks. The way is tricky, but you should enjoy solving the problem.

Small lake at 8198' adorns the east flank of Panoramic Peak.

75

Northeast ridge of East Saint Mary Peak, dusted with mid-September snow. West Saint Mary Peak to the right

On Sunrise Glacier above Turquoise Lake —Cal Tassinari

Lindy Peak 8402 [S] Southeast ridge. The summit has a large meadow with scattered alpine larch. On the summit is a memorial: "In memory of Eugene Prange, missing Sept. 10, 1958. The wind which passes over my dwelling were such as sweep over the mountains bearing the strains of terrestrial music— The morning wind forever blows, but few are the ears that hear it."

West Saint Mary Peak 9372 [S]

East Saint Mary Peak 9425 [S] Southwest spur of southeast ridge, or the steep draw just north of Saint Mary's Lake Dam.

Sonielem Ridge 9315 [S] High point on the northwest end.

Peak Y 9325 [S]

Lowary Peak (Peak X) 9369 [S]

Black Buck Peak 9290 [S] Just south of Lowary Peak

Sunset Peak 8378 [S]

Sunset Crag 8240 [C] Register. Southeast approach. A scramble except for the very top. You may want a rope to rappel. One possible route to watch for goes through a cave.

Gray Wolf Peak 9001 [C] Register. Approaches are unique and exciting. All routes are technical under less than ideal conditions, or when snow is present. Many climbers head into this one early to catch the snow, either in the broad couloir on the south side of the peak, or in the narrow and often icy couloir on the southeast side. Both routes are reached via Riddell Lakes. Start on an old logging road above Twin Lakes and follow a ridgetop approaching Riddell Lakes from the southwest. The south couloir is right above Riddell Lakes. Reaching the southeast couloir involves striking eastward from between Riddell Lakes, feasting on huckleberries as you cross a low spot in the ridge, and swinging left (northward) into Scenic Lakes Cirque. Both couloirs require a rope and ice axe. The southeast couloir has more of a tendency to be icy, but if either one has ice, you'll also want crampons. The southeast couloir is only about 10-20' wide, and usually has a moat on each side. It ends in a notch between the main peak and a false summit on the south end of the mountain. Drop out onto the west side of the mountain (you might want to use your rope here) a couple hundred feet, turn right, and find a break up to the summit. If you go up the broad south couloir, cross over the false summit and drop into the notch at the top of the southeast couloir in order to finish out the climb on the west face.

If you happen to be in Dry Creek you can do the entire climb up the west face. Climb the talus slope into the main couloir. Near the top of this large gully, traverse left to avoid an overhang, then work up into the high broad basin and on to the summit. If you descend the west face, consider

West faces of Glacier Peak (left) and Mountaineer Peak

View from the east of Black Buck Peak (right center) and Lowary Peak (right). Saint Mary Peaks are to the left.

Hiking toward the snow couloir, south side of Gray Wolf Peak
—Cal Tassinari

Close-up of the summits of Lowary Peak (upper left, cairn visible) and Black Buck Peak (foreground)

Looking southeast from Black Buck Peak toward Sunset Crags. Freeman Pass in foreground —U.S. Forest Service

having a rope along for rappelling. This route is an intriguing one to find, and if you do well you'll have no technical difficulties. A more straightforward route is the northeast ridge, another C-rated route which is great if you have a little extra time to get to it. Finally, there is the north ridge, gained by a couloir from No Fish Lake. The couloir ends in an indentation called the Wind Notch, above which technical protection is necessary.

Weather Peak 8227 [S]

Blacktail Peak 8059 [C]

Point 7640 [S] Two miles north of Lower Jocko Lake.

Technical Opportunities: There's a practice area sporting some cliffs just south of Big Fork. It's found above Highway 35, near its junction with Highway 209. Up in the mountains there are broken faces of shale on the higher peaks, including the large Garden Wall. The Sunset Crags have extensive vertical racks. Small features include Eagle Pass Monolith (a gendarme just south of Mt. Harding, easily visible from Highway 93). Also, there are needle formations near Freeman Pass. The rock in the east portion of these is relatively solid, clean, and smooth.

West face of Gray Wolf Peak. A route goes up the main couloir.

A climber above Gray Wolf Lake, poised to strike. Blacktail Peak across the lake
—U.S. Forest Service

78

Camp on the Swan Crest at the head of Pony Creek —Cal Tassinari

The Swan Range

"Often in my dreams, I see the strangest scenes.
I see the mountains rise. I see them touch the skies."

—Jay Ferguson

Description: Sudden and striking—an immediate 6000' rise on the west side, with long ridgetops of grass and timber trailing off eastward. South of Holland Creek the crest is a continuous wall eight miles long. Elsewhere it is set back, less obvious, and broken occasionally by high passes.

Geology: These east-dipping argillite slabs are the same age as those in the Missions but are rugged their entire length. No large glaciers overrode this range, but smaller ones carved out its flanks.

Access: Southeast of Kalispell. Short forest roads from Highway 83 serve trailheads or jumping-off points for steep bushwhacks.

Ownership: Flathead and Lolo national forests.

THE NORTHERN SWAN RANGE

■ **Columbia Mountain 7255 [W]** Turn off Highway 2 about 1¼ miles east of its junction with Highway 40, and head south another ¾ mile to the trailhead. The trail climbs 4100' in a little over four miles. The highest summit is the northern one, in some timber. The central summit, 7234', is the viewpoint. The south summit is 7203'. Heading south on the ridgetop, the trail stays in alpine grass for a couple miles. The east side trail to Hungry Horse has recently become impassable due to overgrowth and downfall. Check the current status of this trail before committing yourself to it.

Columbia Mountain from Columbia Falls

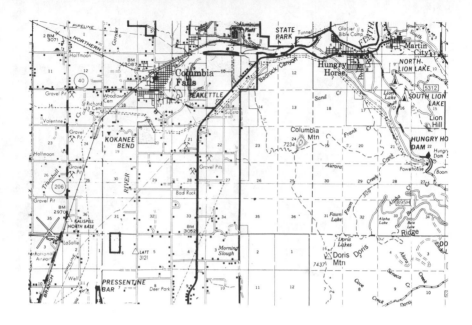

Doris Mountain 7437 [W] Old lookout site.
Blaine Mountain 7207 [S] East side from trail via Jenny Lake.
Hash Mountain 7065 [S] Northeast ridge from trail. This area is quite brushy.
Pioneer Ridge 6479 [W] Old lookout site.

*The Swan Mountains on the east side of
the Flathead Valley. Hash Mountain
and Blaine Mountain at top of photo.
Wildcat Lake at lower right*

80

Mt. Aeneas from the north, above Black Lake

■ **Mt. Aeneas 7530** [W] Turn north off Highway 83, three miles east of its junction with Highway 35, onto the Echo Lake Road. Go 2½ miles to the Noisy Creek Road, a right-hand turn. It's about nine miles to the trailhead at the end of the road. Vehicles with low clearance or questionable brakes should not venture up this road. At the parking lot you can either take the trail to Picnic Lakes and scramble up the east side of the northwest ridge, or walk up the jeep road to its end and take an old tractor trail to the top of the ridge. Once on the ridgetop, just walk up it a mile to the summit.

An interesting man-made addition on the ridge is a microwave site. Years ago, a trailer house containing the installed electronic equipment was dragged up here by tractors in tandem. Soon the wind and heavy snows began to destroy the trailer, so a shelter of cinder blocks was constructed around it. The resulting two-story blockhouse could not be considered inconspicuous, so to make it less offensive a light blue sky and towering mountains were painted on the entire building. It's a fine work of art and serves the purpose as much as can be expected, but it is also one of man's more humorous compromises in the history of wilderness intrusion.

Three Eagles Peak 7462 [S] From the west.

Big Hawk Mountain 7542 [S] West ridge, or the south face up through some brush.

Broken Leg Mountain 7366 [S] Take trail on top of the north ridge for two miles to get close.

Wickiup Mountain 7264 [S] Southwest face, or the southeast ridge.

Mt. Orvis Evans 7450 [S] West or east spurs. Expect brush. This used to be known as Red Owl Peak, but was renamed after a big-wig of the Anaconda Company. Anaconda used to maintain a fancy lodge on Swan Lake for executives.

Sixmile Mountain 7406 [W] Old lookout site.

Hall Peak 6954 [S] This is the rocky tooth seen east of the town of Swan Lake. From Hall Lake bushwhack east to the divide north of the peak, then climb the summit from the northeast.

Con Kelly Mountain 7218 [S] Named for another Anaconda Company chieftain

Kah Point 6385 [J] Old lookout site.

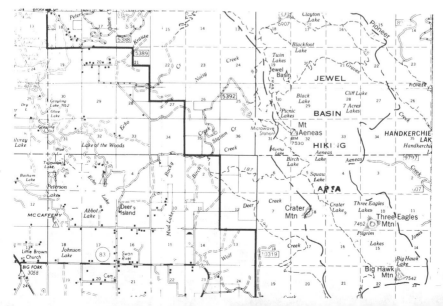

Heading up the west arête to the summit of Swan Peak

The head of Lion Creek, approaching Swan Peak from the southeast —Cal Tassinari

Thunderbolt Mountain 7910 [W] Old lookout site.

Gildart Point 7945 [S] Southwest or northwest ridge from trail. Old lookout site.

THE SWAN FRONT

Napa Point 6423 [D] Old lookout site. This trailhead provides a good view of the Swan Valley.

Inspiration Point 7628 [W] Climb ½ mile up the northeast ridge from trail. Old lookout site.

Swan Peak 9289 [C] Register. There it is, sporting a 6000' elevation rise on its broad shoulders. No quick-and-dirty way from vehicle to mountain, though once there the climb is straightforward. Various wrong ways of getting to this peak are well established. One of the most popular wrong ways is the Squeezer Creek approach, which involves a four-mile bushwhack through alder brush up a trail that doesn't exist. Another route, not quite as wrong, is the ridgetop north of Squeezer Creek, known as the Roller Coaster, which starts at the end of an old logging road and generally follows an elk trail. Several ascents must be made along the ridge, giving an idea of what elk are made of. The grizzly bear in the area are of the same tough wild ingredients, so keep an eye out. This route has scenic qualities making up for the resulting fatigue. You can also wear yourself down on the north ridge, reached from Napa Point or Goat Creek. Take a rope along here. Where the north ridge abuts against the peak, traverse across the northwest face to the west ridge. Finally, you can start by going directly up a long gully northward from Lion Creek to gain access to the west side of the beautiful south ridge. At the top of the ridge, stroll north to some radio transmission equipment, and then notice the sheer cliff blocking your progress to the peak. This is the turn-around point of your outing, unless you want to get technical.

Summit of Swan Peak, Bob Marshall Wilderness in the distance

From Swan Peak southward, small glaciers are flanked by jagged peaks and ridges.

Descending a snowfield in Albino basin
—Cal Tassinari

South ridge of Holland Peak, looking northeast into Dart basin —Cal Tassinari

Now for some legitimate routes. The northeast approach from Sunburst Lake works in late summer after the snow has melted out. Earlier, steep snow and rock makes the climb technical. The best approach is the Squeezer Flank route. Just north of the bridge across Squeezer Creek is a P-rated road. Drive up it through four switchbacks to where it suddenly levels out, then drive to the first creek, where there is a parking spot. Walk northward on the road till past some cliffs in the timber, but no farther than ¼ mile. Then head straight uphill, looking carefully to find a blazed hunter trail. The trail apparently ends halfway up Squeezer Creek canyon in a steep avalanche meadow. At this snow chute drop down 50 yards, relocate the trail and continue on it to the North Fork of Squeezer Creek. There are two lakes up this fork. Gain the west ridge of Swan Peak using either the broad gully from the first lake or the ascending ledge from the second. Once on the ridge, scramble diagonally up the south side of it to a high hanging basin, where the west arete leads up the final 700'.

Longer but not quite as strenuous is the southeast approach. Most of the distance is on the Lion Creek trail, which you leave just where the trail climbs up to Lion Creek Pass. Scramble on up the drainage to a point east of the peak, where an ascending ledge and a short, slightly-exposed stretch complete the route. The upper portion of this route is congested with snow till late summer. Snow may also block your progress on the Squeezer Flank approach till mid-July.

Looking southwest from Holland Peak's summit into the Swan Valley, 5700' below —Cal Tassinari

The Swans in winter. Union Peak to the left —Cal Tassinari

The old Holland Lookout —Cal Tassinari

Summit of Fisher Peak. The summit ridge is gained at the notch left of the top.

Van Peak 8072 [W] Old lookout site. An old trail up the southwest ridge to the top begins from an old logging road near the Lion Creek trailhead.

Union Peak 8825 [C] The west ridge is mostly a scramble, but expect a touch of rock work. The peak can also be reached up the south slope.

Cooney Mountain 8709 [S] North ridge from Smith Creek Pass.

Point 8955 [S] On Holland Peak's northwest ridge. Its west ridge approach is an easy, straightforward route to the top of the Swans.

Holland Peak 9356 [S] Park at Cooney Lookout and hike the trail a mile to its intersection with the old Foothills Trail. Take the right fork (heading south), and in less than ½ mile you'll cross the North Fork of Rumble Creek. About 100 yards past the creek, leave the trail and climb straight up steep slopes through intermittent brush. After gaining a couple thousand feet, the spur begins to level out, and you should be able to find a trail to Lower Rumble Creek Lake. Now head toward the upper lake, staying right when you get near its outlet. Early in the summer a large waterfall can be seen here, even from the highway. If you can see the waterfall, take an ice axe and a rope, because two critical portions of the route most likely still have snow on them. Upper Rumble Creek Lake, at 7900' and ⅓ mile long, is unusually high and large for northwestern Montana. Once on its south shore, head up the slope to the top of the ridge. Until mid-summer there is a large snowbank here and an ice axe is desirable. Once on the ridgetop, climb eastward on it until on the broad south ridge of Holland Peak. The ridge narrows into a sharp saddle below the final grade. When blocked by snow the exposure here is treacherous, and climbers should be roped and belayed. If the snow is gone, just kinda tip-toe across and walk to the top. Really drops down on the west side, doesn't it? Yes, the west face has been climbed, but not very often.

Buck Peak 9003 [S] South ridge. This triangle-shaped peak south of Holland Peak isn't on the Forest Service map.

Looking south along the Swan Crest at Ptarmigan Mountain and Ptarmigan Point, from Wolverine Peak —Cal Tassinari

West face of Fisher Peak

Crescent Mountain, center, from the south

Looking north over Pyramid Pass, Bob Marshall Wilderness beyond. Pyramid Peak in left foreground, Pyramid Pass trail plainly visible —U.S. Forest Service

Holland Lookout Point 8053 [W] This point, northeast of Holland Lake, isn't shown on the Forest Service map. Trail #42, on the map, goes to the spot.

Waldbillig Mountain 8304 [S] Broken route up the west ridge.

Carmine Peak 8542 [S] East face from trail in the saddle west of Little Carmine Peak.

Wolverine Point 8769 [S] Climb the west spur to Point 8535 on the Swan Divide, then head north. The summit is a flat ridge.

Ptarmigan Mountain 8632 [S] Climb the spur just south of Wolverine Peak to Point 8535 on the Swan Divide, then head south.

Ptarmigan Point 9083 [S] Register. Climb the southwest spur to the Swan Crest south of the peak, then walk northward. The crest is broken up near the summit. North of the peak, the crest is also a walk except for a C-rated pitch just below the summit. The west face has an interesting gully (T-rated, wear a rock helmet).

Fisher Peak 8845 [C] Scramble up the steep gully on the west face. Above timberline traverse north out of the gully, then continue up. Near the top, use a chimney adjacent to the arete on the west face at the north end of the summit.

Crescent Mountain 8617 [S] Southwest ridge.

Pyramid Peak 8309 [S] South approach is easiest and most scenic. Leave trail a mile west of Pyramid Pass and head up through beargrass meadows to the western spur of the south ridge. Follow the spur and ridge on up. A quick descent goes down the west ridge or southwest face.

■ **Morrell Mountain 8161** [W] At milepost 15 on Highway 83 in Seeley Lake, turn east onto the Cottonwood Lakes Road and follow it for nine miles to its junction with the Morrell Lookout Road. Climb this road for 8½ miles, parking at the ridgetop just north of the lookout. Walk through open alpine timber over one rise north of the saddle where you parked, then on to the summit. Distance from your car is one mile. At the top you can look out over the Bob Marshall Wilderness. Unless you have your own plane, this climb is by far the easiest way to see the Bob.

Morrell Lookout 7796 [D] Manned lookout building.

THE SOUTH FORK OF THE FLATHEAD RIVER AREA

Oreamnos Peak 7955 [S] 1½ miles west of location shown on Forest Service map.

Stadium Peak 8446 [S]

Marmot Mountain 8250 [S]

Snow Peak 8205 [S]

Brownie Point 8237 [W]

Morrell Mountain from high on its south ridge

The Bob from Morrell Mountain

85

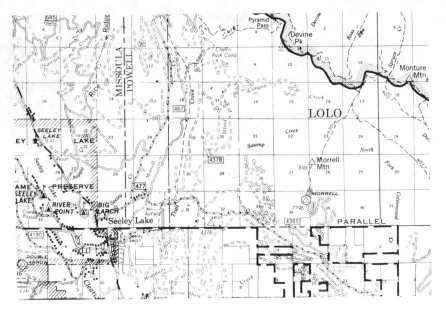

Garnet Peak 8121 [W] Old lookout site.
Charlotte Peak 8079 [W]
Patrol Point 8088 [S]
Lena Peak 8364 [S] Old lookout site.
Scarface Peak 8353 [S]
Una Mountain 8580 [S]
Bullet Nose Mountain 8430 [S]
Kid Mountain 7962 [W] Old lookout site.
Gordon Mountain 8369 [W]
Point 8710 [S] Two miles east of George Lake, at the head of Furious Creek.
Cardinal Peak 8582 [W] Old lookout site.
Count Peak 8691 [S] East peak is highest. North side of mountain quite cliffy.
Goat Mountain 8845 [S] Peak has three summits.
Leota Peak 8512 [S]
Crimson Peak 8281 [S] Most of this climb can be made by trail.
Gust Mountain 8561 [S]
Jumbo Mountain 8284 [W] Old lookout site.
Moser Mountain 8543 [S]
Foolhen Mountain 8535 [W] Old lookout site.
Pinnacle Peak 7725 [S] Southwest ridge.
Little Apex Mountain 7565 [S] Northeast face.
Apex Mountain 7789 [S] Northeast face.
Point 8205 [S] North ridge from Limestone Pass.
Danaher Mountain 8062 [S] South side approach.

86   *North side of Bullet Nose Mountain* —Cal Tassinari   *Goat Mountain on skyline, from the south*

THE MONTURE CREEK AREA

Monture Mountain 8291 [S] Southeast ridge.

Youngs Mountain 8530 [S]

Center Ridge 7071 [W] Old lookout tower at the southeast end of summit ridge.

Fenn Mountain 8241 [W] Old lookout site.

Omar Mountain 8503 [W]

Spread Mountain 8047 [W] The top is ¼ mile off trail in alpine timber. South end of the mountain, 7999', provides a nice vista.

East Spread Mountain 7901 [W] Old lookout tower.

Lake Mountain 8351 [W] Old lookout site.

Ovando Mountain 7799 [S] Southwest ridge.

Technical Opportunities: The Bob Marshall portion of the Swans has lots of shale and limestone cliffs. Most are south of Big Salmon Lake, and are generally concentrated in the Gordon Creek area. The rock is rotten and loose, but the scenery is clean and solid. Closer to home is a nice ice climb up Lost Dog Falls, five miles south of Columbia Falls. Turn east off Highway 2 onto Black Mare Lane, just south of the Midway Store. Access to the ice itself is across private land.

Youngs Mountain (left) and Monture Mountain from the southwest

Morrell Lookout

Open alpine ridgetop northeast of Murphy Peak. Most climbs involve strolling through similar timbered meadows.

McLeod Peak, with the gendarme on its southwest ridge near the left margin

On the summit of McLeod Peak, looking north

The Rattlesnake Mountains

"When you have reached the mountaintop, then you shall begin to climb."
—Kahlil Gibran

Description: A circular isolated range with broken, glaciated high country. Elevation span 5700' on the north side, but elsewhere is more subdued.

Geology: These Precambrian sediments were tightly folded, apparently by larger activities pressing in from all sides. Geologists are waiting for the smoke to clear.

Access: North of Missoula. Back roads serve the south and east portions. Central peaks are attainable only by long trail and cross-country jaunts from Rattlesnake Creek out of Missoula.

Ownership: Lolo National Forest, Flathead Indian Reservation.

Jocko Lookout 7769 [D] A high ridge in the Jocko Wilderness of the Flathead Indian Reservation, open only to members of the Flathead Tribe.

McLeod Peak 8620 [S] No easy way up McLeod. It is isolated—all approaches long or rugged. The southeast ridge is probably easiest, if you already happen to be camped in the upper Rattlesnake. Tribal members can make efficient use of the northeast ridge via Crazy Fish Lake. Long one-day climbs can be made up either Agency Creek or Finley Creek to the west. Finley Creek is unnamed on the Forest Service map, but is just north of Schley Creek. The road (not for cars) is drawn wrong. It starts at the northeast corner of Section 32, not from the highway in Section 31. To climb from Finley Creek, drive up the creek as far as you can, then take the trail to Lower Finley Lake. Go on to the upper lake on the east side of the creek, then head up the not-too-particularly-appealing slopes of broken openings and cliffs to the east. After gaining 1400' you'll

North side of Mosquito Peak, the central mountain in the Rattlesnake

Stuart Peak can be reached by trail from suburban Missoula, in the broad valley south of the peak, in the distance.

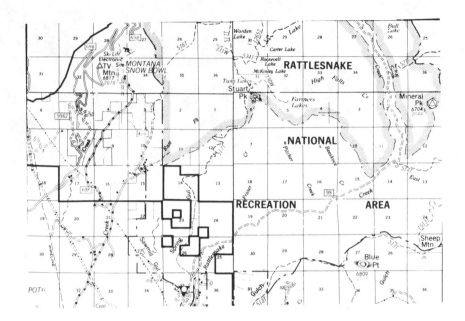

top the ridge. Turn left. Follow the ridgetop as it snakes northeastward. There is a rough, time-consuming stretch of C-rated climbing between Point 8291 and a broken gendarme. You should never have to drop more than ten feet off the jagged ridgetop, blocked here and there by rock outcrops and scrub timber. Go over the gendarme, contour right at the next saddle to skip a high point in the ridge, and take the obvious open route up the south side of McLeod. You can swear by this route, and you can swear at it, but it will get you up and down in a day. It's lots easier to camp out in Rattlesnake Creek, then stroll up from the southeast the next morning.

Gold Creek Peak 7207 [J] Timbered summit and old lookout site, with a good jeep trail down the southeast ridge. A recent burn is off to the northeast.

Murphy Peak 8167 [S] Southwest ridge from Point Six.

Point Six 7929 [W] You could drive your car up here except for the locked gate, which protects radio and weather facilities on the summit. Either walk the road, or come over in winter from the nearby ski area.

TV Mountain 6817 [W] Television transmission towers on the summit. Walk up a gated road, or ski the ridgetop from a ski run.

Mosquito Peak 8057 [W] A small amount of off-trail travel just below the summit.

■ **Stuart Peak 7960** [W] Drive four miles up Van Buren Street from its junction with Interstate 90, and turn left onto the Sawmill Gulch Road. There is a parking area just after you cross Rattlesnake Creek. Hike north up the closed road for ½ mile, then turn left onto the Spring Gulch Trail. It's about 9½ miles to the summit from here. Leave the trail near the top so as to stroll up the northwest ridge. There is alpine scrub on top.

East side of Sheep Mountain

Mt. Jumbo stands east of Rattlesnake Creek at the edge of Missoula.

Mineral Peak 7482 [P] Lookout tower.

Sheep Mountain 7650 [W] Old lookout site. A trail, not on the Forest Service map, goes up Wisherd Ridge from Lockwood Point.

Mt. Jumbo 4768 [S] This 1500' grassy lump rises from Missoula back yards. A steep walk, without benefit of trails, from almost any direction.

Technical Opportunities: High Falls Creek east of Stuart Peak, and Finley Creek southeast of Arlee, have outcrops of the marginal-quality rock interspersed through the range.

A 300' tower of suspect rock up Finley Creek

Main Bitterroot Range—A 60-mile-long series of east-west running ridges

Looking west into the Lolo Peak complex. Carlton Point, right, with northeast peak in the middle above Carlton Lake. The broad summit, left, is highest.

Looking north from Packbox Pass. The central peak is a point on the south ridge of Ranger Peak, visible on the skyline right of it. —U.S. Forest Service

The Bitterroot Mountains

"Rock climbing differs from mountaineering in that the object is not to reach the summit by any or the easiest route but to find the most difficult ways of getting nowhere."
—Warren "Batso" Harding

Description: A dramatic, regularly dissected range. Most streams drain eastward through deep canyons. Rocky jagged summits and extensive rough areas above timberline. Elevation span 6700'.

Geology: This range forms the eastern edge of the Idaho Batholith. 70 million years ago the initial uplift caused the top layers—the Sapphire Block—to slide eastward, exposing granite and metamorphic gneiss (a sedimentary rock recrystallized by heat of adjacent lava). Weather and glaciers eroded all these formations into their present stature.

Access: West of Hamilton. Trails up every major creek leave county roads running west from Highway 93. Logging roads and ridgetop trails serve the southern portion.

Ownership: Bitterroot and Lolo national forests.

Background: Bitterroot ticks are infamous as carriers of Rocky Mountain Spotted Fever. In spring and early summer apply plenty of insect repellent around the openings in your clothes, and check yourself over after the day's activities. If you plan to spend a lot of time here, consider immunizations.

THE LOLO CREEK AREA

West Fork Butte 6157 [D] Manned lookout.
Skookum Butte 7215 [W] Old lookout cabin.
Mormon Peak 6017 [D] Old lookout site. Nice view of Missoula at night.

THE MAIN RANGE

Lolo Peak 9139 [S] Register. Take the north ridge from Carlton Point, 8694', the prominent peak that masks Lolo Peak from Missoula. Carlton Point is reached via Carlton Ridge from a

Northeast side of Saint Joseph Peak

Sweeney Peak from the east

North side of Sky Pilot, Pearl Lake bottom left
—U.S. Forest Service

Canyon Peak's north side

logging road to the east. You can also scramble up from Carlton Lakes, or follow a trail nearly to the top up Lantern Ridge. Lolo Peak actually has two summits, not including Carlton Point. The northeast peak is 9096'. The climb is not too difficult. In fact, it was made by a man aided by crutches in 1922.

Pyramid Buttes 8869 [S] North side. The western point is 8721'.

Sweeney Peak 9161 [S] Southeast ridge.

Saint Joseph Peak 9587 [S] East ridge from Larry Creek, or the southeast ridge. On the east ridge route, when you get to the cliff near the summit, bypass it on the right (north) side if you'd rather scramble up the northeast ridge.

Bass Peak 8855 [S] From the east.

Ranger Peak 8817 [S] South ridge.

Heavenly Twins 9282 [S] Register. South summit is highest, north twin at 9243'. While it is possible to scramble up these peaks, an efficient route will likely involve C-rated climbing. The east ridge is a good approach, and is usually begun at elevation from Saint Mary Peak. Another way is to come up the east side of the north ridge from Kootenai Creek and walk the lofty ridge connecting the two peaks. The hump between the peaks is called The Middle Thing. On the east ridge route, whether approaching from the lookout or from Big Creek, traverse west on the south slope of the high point on the portion of the ridge above Saint Mary Lake. Once in the saddle west of the high point (known as Disappointment Peak), bypass the jagged breaks just east of the summit by traversing onto the south face and into the southeast basin, then up to near the top of the east ridge to finish the climb. There are variants on the east ridge, but all pretty much require heading left onto the south side to avoid obstacles. Some variants need a rope. A route which requires nothing more than mere scrambling has the longest approach to the mountain. Go way up Big Creek, bushwhack up Beaver Creek, then amble up the southwest slopes of the mountain.

East side of the Heavenly Twins, with summit of Saint Mary Peaks in foreground

Castle Crag (upper right) from the northeast. At the lower left are some of the cliffs on the ridgetop south of Fred Burr Creek.

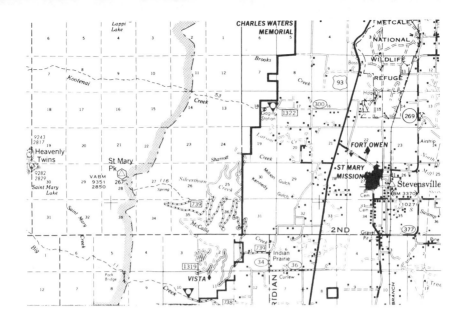

■ **Saint Mary Peak 9351** [W] Turn west off Highway 93 four miles south of the Stevensville turnoff onto the Saint Mary Road. Drive 1¼ miles and take a right turn, then drive another ½ mile to the junction of Forest Road #739. Turn left onto it and climb about 12 miles of switchbacks, then park at the trailhead, 6900'. In a little over three miles the trail climbs 2400' to the broad summit, which has a manned lookout built on a stone foundation. Every summer the Knights of Columbus, a Catholic group, sponsors a religious service here—certainly a suitable spot. This wilderness service is conducted in mid-August, using a rock altar.

Sky Pilot 8792 [S]

Gash Point 8886 [S] From the east.

Castle Crag 8984 [S] Sneak up the back side (south slope or southeast ridge) of this granite tower. Other approaches are technical exercises.

Blodgett Mountain 8648 [S] Southeast face or the east ridge.

Canyon Peak 9155 [T] Rope up at the north col and start up the north ridge. The col can be gained from either side. The route above it alternates between the knife-edged ridge and slab edges on the east face. Some pitons may prove useful. The slabs provide nice belay points, and the moves are not real difficult. You could encounter 5.8, depending on the exact route chosen. Definite exposure is present, and you must be protected. Be equipped to rappel off. Other approaches are harder.

Downing Mountain 8690 [S] Approach from Canyon Creek.

Ward Mountain 9119 [W] Old lookout site.

Whites Mountain 9162 [S] Southeast face.

Koch Mountain 9072 [S] From the south.

Ward Mountain, foreground, El Capitan in the distance

Koch Mountain (far left), Whites Mountain (far right), from the northeast

El Capitan: Southeast ridge and the northeast face

Point 9883. East ridge, left foreground

El Capitan 9983 [S] Southeast ridge, via the saddle northwest of Kerlee Lake. Other approaches are a little steeper but just as interesting and straightforward to scout out. Protection could be desirable on parts of the northeast face, and there are persistent snowbanks on this side of the mountain, although apparently not as persistent as one climber who reportedly did a route up this face with one arm in a sling.

The Lonesome Bachelor 9185 [C] South ridge.

Como Peaks 9624 [S] Three peaks: West Como, the highest; Middle Como, 9530'; and East Como, 9485'. The west and middle peaks are easiest approached from the south, and the east peak from the northeast. The west and middle peaks are scrambles, with perhaps a little C-rated climbing at the very tip-tops. The east peak is a little harder, with the upper portion requiring some careful route finding. Depending on the route chosen, you may desire some protection on the summit pitch, and then descend using a rappel. All three peaks can be approached from either north or south, with simple obvious routes right up to the summit crags.

Point 9883 [S] One mile north of Chaffin Lake. South and east approaches are the easiest. The north side has several technical commitments.

Sugarloaf Peak 9586 [S] Northwest side from Tamarack Lake. The route wanders up huge gullies. The north side involves boulder slopes and couloirs interspersed with snow patches. Expect to spend ages finding the correct route. South and east approaches are technical. The rock there is good, but vertical for as much as 800'.

North Trapper Peak 9801 [T] Register (on middle pinnacle). Take plenty of time to scout out route. A long day by any approach. Consider staying two or three miles from the peak if you camp

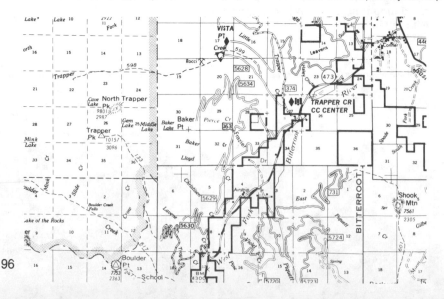

View from the southwest of Como Peaks and Kerlee Lake —U.S. Forest Service

Como Peaks. View from the north of the middle and west peaks

out, since higher campsites have been overused. The peak has been climbed without protection, but it is a good idea to bring a rope for use near the top. Early in the season bring crampons too. They were used by a party on Easter Sunday in 1965. Once on top, the climbers had an Easter egg hunt on the long broken summit. They used the straightforward south couloir route. Head southwest from Trapper Creek up the feeder creek which drains the large cirque southeast of the peak. Look for the couloir, filled with scree once the snow and ice goes out, that stretches diagonally from the scree slopes upward almost to the summit. Near the top of the couloir, rope up and bypass the headwall (sometimes a waterfall) on the left (west) side. A rappel here is convenient on the descent. Above the head of the couloir it's a scramble to the top.

Alternative routes include another large scree (or ice) couloir on the north face, hanging scree slopes and friction slabs on the west face, the southwest ridge from Trapper Peak (difficult route finding, rope needed on one stretch), and the slightly easier northeast ridge.

■ **Trapper Peak 10157** [S] Turn off Highway 93 onto the West Fork Road on the west side of the Bitterroot River Bridge about four miles south of Darby. In about six miles you'll pass the Trapper Creek CC Work Center. Continue on a little over five more miles, then turn right onto the road to the trailhead, about a seven-mile climb for your car. Park and follow the trail onto the broad southeast ridge of Trapper, noting the stands of alpine larch around 8000'. The map shows the trail to the summit, and the route is simple, but expect to lose the trail in the last mile and do some boulder hopping. You can bypass the false summit just east of the main peak. The north side of the peak is steep, and the rock is of comparatively low quality for the area. However, there is a steep ice couloir high in the northeast cirque which can be climbed using crampons. You can use ice screws here, too.

Watchtower Peak 8780 [S] Southeast ridge.

Mt. Jerusalem 9355 [S] Northeast side broken and cliffy.

Bare Peak 9289 [S] From the southwest. Northwest ridge has an unnamed high point of 9349'.

Boulder Peak 9804 [S] South face, or up the east ridge from a lookout.

Boulder Point 7753 [W] Manned lookout.

THE WEST FORK AREA

Medicine Point 8409 [W] Old lookout building.

Piquett Mountain 8831 [W] Old lookout site.

Saddle Mountain 8482 [P] Old lookout site.

Southwest side of North Trapper Peak, with part of the west ridge of Trapper peak in the foreground

Trapper Peak, looking into the large cirque on its northeast side

Northeast side of Boulder Peak (upper right)

Mountaintops in the West Fork are often covered with alpine grasses and scattered clumps of whitebark pine.

Bare Cone 7822 [D] Manned lookout.

Steep Hill 7977 [S] Northeast ridge from trail.

Blue Joint Point 8681 [S] Short scramble from a trail to the east, in a corner of the state line. This point is ½ mile east of Blue Joint Hill in Idaho.

Razorback Mountain 8637 [W]

Deer Creek Point 8367 [W] Old lookout site.

Lookout Mountain 7830 [D] Manned lookout.

Thunder Mountain 7699 [W] Old lookout site.

Allan Benchmark 8909 [W] On the state line ten miles southwest of Lost Trail Pass.

Blue Nose Mountain 8677 [J] Old lookout building.

Johnson Point 8718 [W] On the state line, three miles east of Blue Nose Mountain.

Technical Opportunities: Although the rock is not good by regional standards, it provides the best and most accessible climbing in western Montana. The rock at its finest is quartz monzonite granite, in a wide assortment of formations ranging from boulders and cute little pinnacles to vertical faces of ten or more pitches. The rock is old and fractured, and, while being less than perfect, does provide plenty of ways to install protection without the use of bolts. Bolts have been used for practice, and on some inconspicuous friction slabs, but have usually been left home instead on significant routes. The local climbers have taken care of the rock, and have usually retreated off a route until a way could be found to do it without bolts. This is a nice precedent, and there is no pressure in the Bitterroots to put up a specific first ascent—there are always plenty of other routes waiting to be pioneered. No one keeps track anyway.

West side of Gash Ridge Needles
—U.S. Forest Service

Spire up Fred Burr Creek
—U.S. Forest Service

98

Chief Charlo in the Ramparts of Kootenai Creek

Shoshone Spire in Blodgett Creek

Lolo Hot Springs: Granite boulders are situated along the highway and up the East Fork of Lolo Creek.

Bass Creek Crags: Formations, including Sawtooth Ridge, The Turret, and Mickey Mouse, are concentrated above Lappi Lake. Other nearby formations are on the south side of Bass Creek. Also, there's a waterfall in this drainage that ices up well in winter.

Kootenai Creek: This area is popular because of its proximity to Missoula, even though the rock is gneiss and schist. Formations are at the mouth of the canyon north of the creek. The gneiss bands tilt eastward, so there are poor handholds on east faces but good ones on south and west faces. Practice rocks and cliffs, including the popular Easter Rock, are ½ mile up the trail, north of the diversion dam. About 1000' above these formations are the Ramparts, a series of west-facing cliffs on staggered buttresses. The fourth one up has two good routes. The southwest ridge route can be well protected with nuts. The Chief Charlo route, a 5.6 or 5.7 effort, starts on the west face in an obvious chimney and finishes with an exposed crawl under the overhanging roof of the summit. There are no significant formations on up the creek. Please don't disturb eagle nests when climbing in the area.

Big Creek: On the north side of the creek, just below Big Creek Lake, is a massive series of long arêtes.

Small natural arch, Blodgett Creek. Rappels are made directly off the apex.

Leading a pitch about ⅓ of the way up —Marvin McDonald

1000' fractured granite face stands nearly vertical and is the tallest formation in the canyon. —Marvin McDonald

Gash Ridge: The Gash Ridge Needles and associated cliffs are northwest of Gash Point at the head of Sweathouse Creek.

Bear Creek: There's a friction rock practice area between the North and Middle forks of Bear Creek. Note: In Bear Creek and all the drainages to the south as far as the Nez Perce Fork of the Bitterroot River, hidden cliffs and unusual formations are all over the place.

Fred Burr Creek: There are spires on the north side of the creek about two or three miles up the trail. Remember property rights, as the initial trail access is across private land.

Mill Creek: There are rocks to practice on ½ mile up the trail. The ridge north of the creek has some spires. A 5.9 free climb can be made up No Sweat Arête toward the west end of the spires.

Resting on a belay ledge —Marvin McDonald

Blodgett Creek: There is a concentration of truncated spurs lining the north side of this canyon. Most direct routes up these are consistently 5.8-5.9. The first two formations, The Prow and Stegasaurus Ridge, are dark-colored metamorphic rock and seem to have more than their share of accidents.

Then comes a series of four light-colored granitic buttresses. The first is Blackfoot Dome, known also as The Beehive. This feature is made to order for those who are not sure of themselves. The southeast side is easy and gets progressively more difficult as one angles to the left (west). One can simply zig-zag in the slabs and ledges to find the desired challenge and exposure. There's also a zig-zag route up the difficult south face, but it wanders by necessity, not choice. Nuts work well in the shallow cracks of this formation.

Blackfoot Dome is actually the lower of three formations attached like stairs up the hillside, angling west. On the middle formation, Kootenai Buttress, one encounters a 5.8 smooth slab after doing the central open-book chimney. The route wanders all over the south face, providing all types of climbing. An easier climb starts 100' or so east of the open book. Both the Kootenai and Blackfoot formations have escape routes. This is not so on the three remaining buttresses to the west, where rappels are necessary to retreat.

The next one up the canyon is Nez Perce Buttress. The right side of the face has smooth friction slabs, not always easy to place protection on. The left side of the face is harder, with four pitches of 5.8-5.9 for a long day. Some climbers take two days.

The third granitic buttress in the canyon, Shoshone Spire, is less time-consuming if one does the 600' southwest arête. This interesting route begins with open books and jam cracks, steepening into rounded holds and overhangs. The route is often finished by moving around onto the west face. Pitons and etriers are helpful. The south face of Shoshone is a sheer 800', with fierce overhangs ⅔ of the way up.

Most imposing is Flathead Buttress, the fourth of the big buttresses. Take pitons, nuts, and time. There's a lot of 5.6, upward to maybe 5.10 depending on the route chosen. There's an open book up the middle, reached by starting in a corner on the right-hand side of the face, then traversing left on ledges. Another route, 5.7 minimum, goes up the west corner of the face. Both routes require about eight pitches. The face can be climbed in a day, but usually by climbers who have first-hand knowledge of their route by prior reconnaissance.

Just past Flathead, recessed up the hill, is Beaverhead Buttress, also known as Mandan Ridge. There's an open book on the southwest corner, and a 5.7 route on the west face traversing back and forth on small ledges. Trees are sometimes used for protection. The summit is sharp and serrated

Those are the major features. Smaller formations are scattered about, including a triangular friction slab across the canyon from Shoshone Spire, and a small natural arch also on the south side. Higher up on Romney Ridge are large sheer cliffs. In winter, waterfalls often ice up. One is between Nez Perce and Shoshone.

Canyon Creek: Nice towers are on the north side of the creek.

South Fork Lost Horse Creek: A long series of truncated spurs are on the ridge to the north.

Rock Creek: One large granite spur stands on the creek on the north side.

Trapper Peak Area: Formations include outcrops in Trapper and Boulder creeks, spires west of Trapper Peak, and a pinnacle above Crow Creek south of Trapper Peak. There's a snow gully on the east side of this pinnacle, and also one above Gem Lake.

Looking north from Kent Peak

Mt. Sentinel, 2000' above Missoula. The "M" is 800' up.

Summit of Dome Shaped Mountain—good place for a picnic

The Sapphire Mountains

"They shall call the people unto the mountain; there they shall offer sacrifices of righteousness."

—Deuteronomy 33:19

Description: A broad massive plateau with dramatic hidden valleys. Most summits covered by meadows or open alpine timber. Elevation span 5300'.

Geology: When the Idaho Batholith to the west uplifted, the Sapphire Block (thick sedimentary layers) slid eastward.

Access: South of Missoula. Logging roads from perimeter highways cover most of the range. Major routes include the Skalkaho Pass Road (Highway 38) and the Rock Creek Road (Highway 348). Trails are on all unroaded ridges.

Ownership: Lolo, Bitterroot, and Deerlodge national forests.

Mt. Sentinel 5158 [W] There is a trail up the northwest flank from the University of Montana, 3200'. A jeep trail approaches the peak from the southeast. (The east ridge drops and then continues to gain elevation, but you soon lose a great view of the Missoula valley. There is an aircraft beacon at 5806'.) Mt. Sentinel has always been a popular climb with Missoulians and students. The Montana Mountaineers held their first meeting on its summit on August 5, 1922.

Mt. Dean Stone 6203 [S] Walk old roads from Pattee Canyon or climb directly up the northwest spur.

Miller Peak 7030 [D] Radio facilities. Old lookout site.

Cleveland Mountain 7337 [W]

Welcome Point 7723 [W]

Sliderock Mountain 7820 [P] Radio facilities. Old lookout site. The building is now at Fort Missoula.

Quigg Peak 8419 [W] Old lookout site.

Point 8480 [S] Noted on Forest Service map as "Peak 2 miles east of Quigg." Easiest way is to scramble ⅛ mile up the northeast ridge from trail.

Dome Shaped Mountain from ridgetop trail a mile south

Southeast from the Sapphire Divide. Mt. Emerine to the left in the middle distance, Anaconda Range on skyline

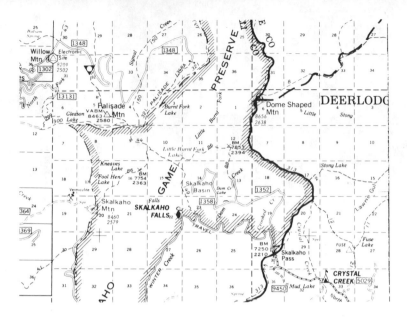

Willow Point 7787 [W] On Sandstone Ridge.

Sand Point 8272 [W] A flat timbered point on Sandstone Ridge.

Silver King Point 7851 [W]

Black Pine Ridge 7937 [D] Old lookout site. The actual lookout building is now at the Smoke Jumper Center in Missoula.

Willow Mountain 8209 [D] Manned lookout. Radio facilities.

Palisade Mountain 8463 [W] Old lookout site.

■ **Dome Shaped Mountain 8660** [W] Drive Highway 38 from Hamilton or Philipsburg to Skalkaho Pass. Either take the trail out of the pass northward for six miles, or take the road which climbs north out of the west side of the pass and follow it about four miles to a road junction in a logged area. Turn right (north) and go about ⅔ mile to where the road crosses Dam Creek in Section 13. Trail #88 doesn't appear to exist, unless it's been reopened since 1981, so park at the creek crossing and hike upstream along the south side of the creek. Continue in the same direction once above the head of the channel, crossing several game trails until you get to the pack trail on the ridgetop. It's two miles on the trail to the broad summit. The distance from your vehicle to the ridgetop trail is one mile, so a little cross-country travel, instead of taking the trail from Skalkaho Pass, cuts your hiking distance in half.

Skalkaho Mountain 8460 [W]

Gird Point 7715 [W] Old lookout building and heliport. Short walk up trail from car road.

Practice cliff in Hellgate Canyon, south side of Clark Fork River, ½ mile east of Missoula

104   *Fox Peak (left) and Congdon Peak (center) from the southwest*

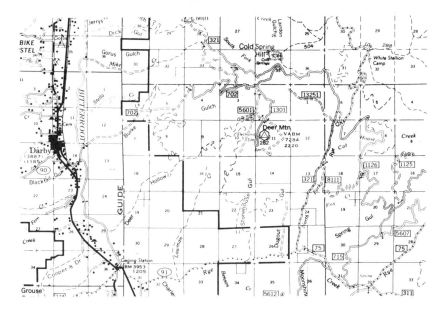

Mt. Emerine 8639 [S] Trail and old jeep trail to old lookout site on the north peak, 8616'.

Black Bear Point 7537 [D]

Bald Top Mountain 7355 [W] Old lookout site.

Fox Peak 8796 [S] South or northwest ridge from trail.

Congdon Peak 8884 [S] Southwest or north ridge. Forest Service map shows trail to summit. Trail apparently a little west of where drawn.

Kent Peak 8999 [S] From Coyote Meadows the trail is a fireline along a ridgetop, on the edge of logging. After reaching a high point on the ridge, watch for a large rock outcrop on the next high point of the ridge. Just before the outcrop, but past a grassy opening, is where the foot trail leaves the fire trail. For 1½ miles the trail is plain enough, and its junction with the trail that heads down past Kent Lake is easy to find. Take the trail into the Kent Lake cirque, dropping through forests of alpine larch, and, when at the level of the lake, leave the trail and head through the woods for the lake. The trail goes way below the lake and is drawn wrong on the new Forest Service maps. Get around to the east side of the lake and climb through a timbered break in the line of cliffs. Now angle north and ascend boulder slopes to a boulder peak just north of the main peak, and follow the connecting ridge.

Bare Hill 8750 [S] Southeast ridge from trail.

■ **Deer Mountain 7284** [D] Turn east off Highway 93 onto the Rye Creek Road five miles south of Darby and go about six miles to a road junction. Take Road #321, a left turn, and go a little over 4½ miles to the next road junction, but stay on the main road for another seven miles. By this time you should be seeing road signs directing you to the mountain at every questionable junction. On top is a manned lookout tower and some radio facilities.

Blue Mountain 7451 [D] Road #5778 crosses this summit.

Sula Peak 6191 [P] Manned lookout.

McCart Point 7115 [W] Old lookout. Short trail hike from car road.

Technical Opportunities: There's not much rock climbing up high, although a winter trip to Skalkaho Falls could be an ice-climber's delight. There are practice cliffs in the lower drainages. Hellgate Canyon, ½ mile east of the University of Montana, has an 80' 80-degree cliff with ample handholds for beginners. This face can be top-roped for complete protection. For a different type of climbing try Redtail Rocks, volcanic tuff formations up the first creek east of the Ravenna railroad tunnel, about seven miles east of Rock Creek. Most of these formations can also be top-roped. Take the Rock Creek freeway exit to get on the south side of the river. On up Rock Creek itself, flimsy cliffs and towers flank the streambank in the Squaw Rock area. If you'll settle for nothing less than stiff granite, try the formations at Dalles Campground.

Long eastern slopes, Deer Lodge Valley

Pikes Peak Ridge from the northeast (right) and Dolus Creek (center). Pikes Peak hidden behind the ridge, at the head of Dolus Creek

East side of Trask Point

The Flint Creek Range

"We were in such an airy elevation above the creeping population of the earth that it seemed that we could look around and abroad and contemplate the whole great globe."

—Mark Twain

Description: Compact and somewhat hidden behind its own sloping fringes, but with a 6100' elevation gain. Broad inclines of grass and timber surround a cluster of peaks consisting of fractured rock and boulder fields.

Geology: The sliding Sapphire Block bulldozed up sedimentary strata on its leading edge to form this range. Granite came up through the resulting folds. Little is visible; outcrops were probably scoured off by glaciation.

Access: West of Deer Lodge. Roads and jeep trails climb from all perimeter highways, with most approaches made from Interstate 90.

Ownership: Deerlodge National Forest.

Mt. Princeton 7919 [S] Short scramble from nearby pack trails, or from jeep trail.

Pikes Peak 9359 [S] Head up the northeast cirque from Pikes Peak Ridge (the peak's northeast ridge), or scramble onto the shorter east ridge from Dolus Lake.

Goat Mountain 9283 [S] South ridge, gained via the east bowl from Upper Goat Mountain Lake (above Thompson Lake).

Racetrack Peak 9522 [S] Try the east shoulder from Racetrack Pass. Can also climb from the west.

■ **Mt. Powell 10168** [S] Take the county road which heads west from downtown Deer Lodge. In two miles go straight rather than take the left turn to the State Prison. In four more miles a primitive road heads left (west). Take it, and then in two miles take the left-hand fork just past the power line. On the Forest Service map this is Road #5149, and is pretty much for four-wheel-drive vehicles. Follow it five miles to the end, where it fades out in a meadow after following the top of a broad ascending ridge and then dropping onto its south side. Hike the trail about four miles, almost to Martin Lake, then turn left (east) onto the bouldery northwest buttress of Mt. Powell. On the way up this buttress you'll notice old telephone poles set in cairns. There used to be a lookout atop the buttress, with communications provided by a heavy bare telephone wire. Once there, simply walk the ridge south to the summit, where there is a register. Another route is the south ridge, obtained from a long jeep trail in Dempsey Creek, beginning from the State Prison Ranch.

Deer Lodge Mountain 9765 [S] Northeast ridge from Morrison Gulch—South America Park.

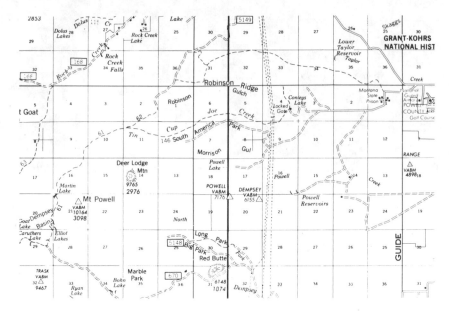

Trask Point 9467 [S] East ridge.
Red Lion Point 8773 [S] Southwest shoulder.
Twin Peaks 9067 [S] North side. East peak 8977'.
Cable Mountain 8119 [P] Old lookout site.

Technical Opportunities: There are no special attractions, just the usual scattered broken faces. At the Granite Mine, four miles east of Philipsburg, are a small amount of bouldering opportunities. The northeast side of Mt. Powell (just under the summit) has a fractured cliff a few hundred feet high with plenty of handholds and loose rocks. Bring a rock helmet.

Mt. Powell (left) and Deer Lodge Mountain are connected by a long ridge. View from the east

East wall of Peak 10259
overlooks Warren Lake.
—U.S. Forest Service

The Anaconda Range

"Every start upon an untrodden path is a venture which only in unusual circumstances looks sensible and likely to be successful."

—Albert Schweitzer

Description: Higher peaks arranged at the northeast end of an expanse of alpine timber and rocky slopes. Elevation span 6300'. On most peaks the scenery is of higher quality than the rock.

Geology: These mountains formed on the leading edge of the irrepressible Sapphire Block. Granitic intrusions poked through the folded strata, and are exposed on Warren Peak.

Access: South of Anaconda. Trails from forest roads in the lower drainages cross the crest of the range. The larger peaks can be reached from the Middle Fork Rock Creek Road, which leaves Highway 38 ten miles west of Highway 10A.

Ownership: Deerlodge, Bitterroot and Beaverhead national forests.

Johnson Point 8880 [W]
Bender Point 8439 [W] Old lookout site.

Tamarack Lake cowers under the northwest face of Warren Peak. —U.S. Forest Service

Looking southwest from Storm Lake Pass on Mt. Tinys' southeast rige. Queener Mountain on center skyline —U.S. Forest Service

Mt. Haggin as most people see it, from northeast of Anaconda

Senate Mountain 8764 [S] East face.

West Pintler Peak 9498 [S] Register. South face from nearby trail, or the north ridge.

East Pintler Peak 9486 [S] Southeast ridge from Pintler Pass.

Peak 9805 [S] Just south of Martin Lake. Come at it from anywhere except the lake.

Warren Peak 10464 [S] The southwest slope from Edith Lake is easiest. However, C-rated routes on the granitic north or east faces are more popular. One option is to go up the north face until difficulties are encountered, then swing onto the east side. After skirting cliffs, weasel up to open slopes on the northeast shoulder and the summit. Technical routes, including a snow couloir (take ice axe) are on the north side of the mountain.

Peak 10259 [S] Southwest ramp. Technical possibilities on the east and north faces (1200' wall on the north side).

West Goat Peak 10793 [S] Northwest ridge from saddle just south of Warren Lake. A long steep stroll with no obstacles.

East Goat Peak 10399 [S] This and West Goat Peak are known collectively as Saddle Mountain.

Marche Point 9823 [W] Southwest ridge. The trail from Cutaway Pass goes within a few hundred feet of the top.

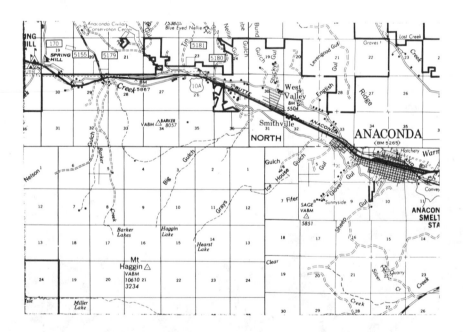

Fish Peak 10240 [S] West ridge from Cutaway Pass.

Queener Mountain 10149 [S] Northwest ridge.

Mt. Tiny 9848 [S] Short scramble up the southeast ridge from Storm Lake Pass.

Mt. Howe 10472 [S]

Mt. Evans 10641 [S] Northeast or southeast ridges.

■ **Mt. Haggin 10610** [S] From Anaconda drive west on Highway 10A to the end of the four-mile straight stretch, and then three more miles to the Barker Creek turnoff. It's then five miles south to Barker Lakes. From the lakes, scramble up a north spur to the west ridge, and then eastward to the top. This is the shortest way, depending on how far your truck can get up the Barker Creek Road. If going up via Hearst Lake, a gully on the northeast side of the peak is one option.

Grassy Mountain 8018 [P] Maintained lookout.

Technical Opportunities: Exposed granite around Warren Peak provides quality climbing. The extreme faces and spires around Peak 10259 are of mixed rock and could prove interesting, depending on your preference. Around the Warren Lake-Rainbow Lake area are granite boulders scattered through the woods. None are very big, but can be used for bouldering in an exceptionally pristine environment.

Northwest view of Mt. Haggin, showing the west ridge and the north spur that comes up to it from Barker Lake

Torrey Mountain (right), and granite spires on the divide between David and Elkhorn creeks

Southeast side of Mt. Fleecer

The Pioneer Mountains

"Sophisticated equipment and the natural features of the rock may help, but ultimately climbing is a lonely job."

—Burt Peters

Description: A very diverse range, split by the Wise River. West half subdued and timbered. East half rugged, with broken talus domes, jagged peaks, and 5700' elevation span over high valleys.

Geology: Undetermined. Geologists speculate these sedimentary layers slid east from the Big Hole Valley. Lava intruded from below, resulting in massive granitic outcrops in the heavily glaciated East Pioneers. Less glacial activity in the West Pioneers. The extreme north end of the range is on the western edge of the Boulder Batholith.

Access: Southwest of Butte. Forest Highway #484 from Wise River to Highway 278 bisects the range and provides access to both halves via short roads and good trails.

Ownership: Beaverhead National Forest, Butte District Bureau of Land Management on the fringes.

THE NORTH PIONEERS

Sugarloaf Mountain 7766 [W] From the east.

Burnt Mountain 8383 [S] Leave Fleecer Ridge trail from the south when near the peak.

Dickie Peak 9116 [S] Southwest ridge.

Little Granulated Mountain 9062 [S] ½ mile from trail on the east side. Grassy summit.

Granulated Mountain 9157 [S] Trail on the west side a mile from talus summit.

Mt. Fleecer 9436 [S] North ridge or southwest slope from jeep trails.

THE WEST PIONEERS

Foolhen Mountain 9088 [W]

Alder Peak 9210 [W] Old lookout.

Round Top Mountain 9345 [S] From the east. A timbered dome.

Stine Mountain 9497 [S] North ridge from trail.

Bobcat Mountain 9241 [S] South ridge from trail.

■ **Odell Mountain 9446** [W] Turn west off Forest Road #484 about 18 miles south of Wise River and drive four miles to the end of the Lacy Creek Road. Park and hike up the well-maintained Pioneer Loop Trail 4½ miles to Schwinegar Lake. The trail parallels the east shore to the north end of the lake. Here an old trail takes off to the left (west), immediately climbing a ridge. It's steep and overgrown in spots. Look for old blazes. Within one mile you'll see the northeast side of Odell Mountain. The trail will be a little harder to find, but skirts the east base of the mountain through open timber and grassy slopes. On the southeast side of the mountain, find a set of switchbacks up

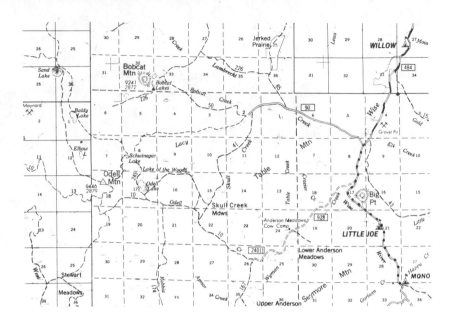

the east side of the peak to the L-shaped plateau. On the actual summit is an old lookout foundation and log storehouse.

Trails also approach the summit from Steel Creek, but don't expect them to be in better shape than the one above Schwinegar Lake.

Deer Peak 9165 [S] From the northwest.

THE EAST PIONEERS

Black Lion Mountain 10428 [S] Southwest peak is the highest. The other summit, 10418', is shown on the Forest Service map. Try the south ridge or southeast ramp.

Granite Mountain 10633 [S] Northeast ridge from Granite Lake, or the south side.

Storm Peak 9494 [W] Grassy top.

Mt. Tahepia 10473 [S] Composed of broken granite. Head up the east ridge from Waukena Lake, the north side, or the west ridge from Schulz Lake.

Comet Mountain 10212 [S] Scramble from the Gar Mine high on the west side.

Tweedy Mountain 11154 [S] Register. The east side from Barb Lake, or the north side from Gorge Lakes are tedious but direct scrambles. From Torrey Lake, there are two good ways up to the south ridge. One heads up a long talus chute just to the right of the peak. The other is south of the chute, heading up the green slopes between the gray- and rust-colored rocks. The west ridge starts out easily enough but is difficult just under the flat summit. The ridge traverse between Tweedy Mountain and Torrey Mountain is technical granite.

Barb Mountain 10497 [S] Scramble up the east side. The connecting ridge to Tweedy Mountain shouldn't be attempted without rock climbing gear.

Torrey Mountain 11147 [S] Register. A long scramble from the east, or from Lily Lake to the southeast. The approach from Torrey Lake is via the northeast ridge, gained by C-rated climbing.

North from Odell Mountain. Bobcat Mountain, center of photo

Northeast side of Odell Mountain

East Pioneers from the east side of Odell Mountain

Thunderhead blossom over the southern West Pioneers

Important: The huge boulder slide above the south shore of Torrey Lake shifted in 1981 and is still very unstable. Be careful, as the steeper sections of rubble can completely give out under you. Traverse upward across this slide toward the notch on the ridge. When almost there, angle right, climbing steep broken outcrops to the broad saddle south of the notch.

Call Mountain 9019 [S] Road on the north side. Low profile peak with a nice little grassy park.

Sugarloaf Mountain 8892 [S] North ridge. Grassy top.

Twin Adams Mountain 8165 [S] Short scramble from a mine road. Timbered top.

Thunderhead Mountain 8236 [S] West approach. Timbered top.

Sawtooth Mountain 10294 [S] Northeast shoulder from Anchor Lake. South ridge is technical.

Highboy Mountain 10431 [T] North face of the east buttress, above Tub Lake (good rock), and the north ridge. All approaches finish with exposed rock on the summit pitch.

Tent Mountain 10193 [S] Northeast ridge from Mule Creek. A little C-rated climbing on the south approach.

Tweedy Mountain and Torrey Lake

Torrey Lake and the north face of Torrey Mountain

The final 1000' of the northeast ridge of Torrey Mountain under stormy skies

West side of the southern East Pioneers, from Comet Mountain (left) to Alturas No. 2

West side of Baldy Mountain

Alturas #2 Mountain 10550 [S] North or east ridges. "Altura" is Spanish for altitude or a high point.

Alturas #1 Mountain 10153 [S] Northeast, northwest, or south ridge.

Baldy Mountain 10568 [S] The south face is the closest side to a road, although the top can be reached from any side. Lookout cabin.

Tower Mountain 9268 [S] Old lookout site. A mining road gets within ¼ mile of the summit.

Humbolt Mountain 9213 [S]

Dutchman Mountain 7334 [S] Southwest swale.

Technical Opportunities: For practice, there's a 300' cliff on the west side of the Wise River, just under eight miles from the town of Wise River. The cliff has an open book and a chimney. The southern portion of the East Pioneers has probably the most significant untested concentration of technical granite in Montana. These remote, heavily fractured formations stretch from just south of Mt. Tahepia to the Tent Mountain area. Tweedy and Torrey mountains have arêtes and spires on their west sides. More spires are concentrated on the divide between Elkhorn and David creeks, dominated by a large clean-looking white gendarme.

Point 10209 on Torrey Mountain's west ridge, a typical granite spire of the East Pioneers

The twin granite spires of Tweedyl-dee and Tweedyl-dum, on Tweedy Mountain's south ridge

Northeast view of Point 10388, easternmost of the Lima Peaks

East ridge route on Homer Youngs Peak. Left: Looking west toward the peak from just above timberline. Right: The final portion of the ridge from the saddle above Rock Island Lakes

The Beaverhead Mountains

"When man feels the wind blowing through him on a high peak or sleeps under closely matted whitebark pine in an exposed basin, he is apt to find his relation to the universe."

—William O. Douglas

Description: A long range, with gradual ramps approaching the peaks from the east. Exposed rock and alpine timber in the north. Grassy in the south, with a 5800' elevation span. (The broad nature of the range disguises any immediate drops of that magnitude.) To the west are the dry valleys and ranges of Idaho, whose influence is apparent in the southern portion of the Beaverheads, where drinking water is not readily found.

Geology: A block of strata uplifted along faults on either side and weathered into its present configuration. Granitics are in the main range, with Precambrian sediments in the Tendoys. There was volcanic activity west of Monida Pass.

Access: West of Dillon. County and ranch roads in the major valleys originate from Interstate 15 and Highway 278. Jeep and foot trails reach into the uplands.

Ownership. Beaverhead National Forest, Butte District Bureau of Land Management.

THE NORTHERN CONTINENTAL DIVIDE AREA

Sheep Mountain 9858 [S] Northeast or southeast ridge.

Pyramid Peak 9616 [S] Northeast or southeast ridge.

Squaw Mountain 10404 [S] East ridge.

Ajax Peak 10028 [S] Gain the south ridge from Ajax Lake. The east ridge has a little C-rated climbing.

Point 10042 [S] Gain the west ridge from Ajax Lake. This peak is just south of the Ajax mine.

Looking north from the summit of Homer Youngs Peak into the Big Hole Valley. Squaw Mountain on the left skyline

Looking south from Homer Youngs Peak across Rock Island Lake toward Monument Peak and Center Mountain

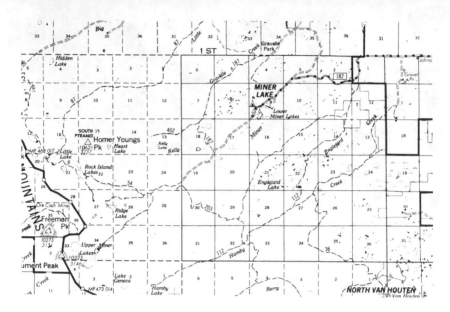

Homer Youngs Peak 10621 [S] Turn west off Highway 278 on to Forest Road #182 ½ mile south of Jackson and follow it 11 miles to Miner Lake. Park here unless you have a four-wheel drive, which will get you 2½ miles farther up Miner Creek, where you'll park at the road closure sign. Walk northward from there across the open area and hike straight up the open timber to the top of the east ridge of Homer Youngs Peak. Simply follow the open ridge westward three miles. Other routes include hopping onto the east ridge just after crossing Kelly Creek, going up the northeast ridge from Little Lake Creek, or heading northeast from the foot of Lower Rock Island Lake straight up the mountainside to the large saddle just southeast of the peak. The Rock Island Lake route is longer and encounters more loose rock than the east ridge route, but provides a quick, scenic descent. From the summit you'll see two pointed peaks to the southwest. These are Copperhead Peak and Freeman Peak, both C-rated, over in Idaho.

Monument Point 10323 [C] North ridge. East face rated T. This point is labeled Monument Peak on the maps, but that summit is 1½ miles south. Monument Point is merely a scramble from the Idaho side.

Monument Peak 10390 [C] North ridge from Monument Point. East face is broken and steep. Like Monument Point, just a scramble from the Idaho side.

Center Mountain 10362 [S] Gain the southeast ridge from the head of Berry Creek.

Selway Mountain 8898 [W] Old lookout site.

Bloody Dick Peak 9817 [S] Old lookout site, with little left of the trail that served it.

Tash Peak 9348 [S] East side.

Badger Point 7508 [S] Just south of Badger Pass on Highway 278.

THE SOUTHERN CONTINENTAL DIVIDE AREA

Jeff Davis Peak 9599 [S] West ridge.

Maiden Peak 10227 [S] Eastern approach using trail up Schwartz Creek.

Horse Prairie Point 10194 [S] Northeast or southeast ridge.

Center Mountain's outstretched ridges enhance the Big Hole Valley.

Northeast ramp of Eighteenmile Peak. No two mountains in Montana are alike, and this peak is one that exemplifies that diversity.

The westernmost of the Lima Peaks

Red Conglomerate Peaks (right), with Knob Mountain (left)

Bear Point 9594 [W] You may be able to get a jeep up the trail.

Baldy Mountain 10773 [S] East side up Lake Gulch.

Eighteenmile Peak 11141 [S] Register. Northeast ramp approach from Harkness Lakes, a prairie ascent. Slopes of grass and sage extend past 10000', and antelope are often seen that high. A four-wheel drive can sometimes make it to the springs up Bear Creek. From the summit one can see the dry grassy hills in Montana, lush compared to the dusty desert in the Lemhi Valley of Idaho. Eighteenmile Peak is the highest point on the Continental Divide in Montana and on the Montana-Idaho state line.

Italian Peak 10998 [S] Gain the northwest ridge from the Nicholia Creek Trail. This peak is connected by a two-mile-long ridge with Scott Peak, 11393', in Idaho.

Garfield Mountain 10961 [S] South shoulder from Little Sheep Creek. Actually, this peak is easy from any side.

Lima Peaks 10706 [S] These three peaks can be approached via the east ridge, or on one of the northern spurs, or many other easy ways. The three summits from the west to east are: 10706', 10060', 10388'.

Red Conglomerate Peaks 10106 [S] Leave the trail and climb over a knob on the northeast ridge (not Knob Mountain). This peak trails off into Idaho. You could encounter C-rated climbing, depending on the route chosen.

East side of Timber Butte

East side of Dixon Mountain

THE TENDOY MOUNTAINS

This small range consists mostly of broad grassy ridges. Most of the trails shown on the Forest Service map are jeep trails. The P-rated road up Sourdough Creek climbs to 9380' near Sourdough Cave.

Sourdough Peak 9571 [J] Extensive grassy hilltop.

Timber Butte 9472 [S] Southwest ridge from jeep trail.

Dixon Mountain 9674 [S] North or south ridge, or the west spur from Trail #82.

Technical Opportunities: Other than a short pitch of firm rock in the peaks west of the Big Hole Valley, the rock is not specifically too good, although formations do reach significant size. Typical formations are the limestone cliffs in Big Sheep Creek Canyon, and Pipe Organ Rock southwest of Dillon on the west side of Interstate 15.

Limestone cliffs in Big Sheep Creek provide limited climbing opportunities.

Wall Creek Cliffs east of Silvertip Mountain

The Flathead Range

"Have you gazed on naked grandeur where there's nothing else to gaze on,
Set pieces and drop-curtain scenes galore,
Big mountains heaved to heaven which the blinking sunsets blaze on,
Black canyons where the rapids rip and roar?"

—Robert Service

Description: A sprawling range of long ridges and walls flanked by deep canyons. Peaks are broken outcrops on extensive talus slopes, surrounded by large alpine basins. Elevation span 5600'.

Geology: This is the central portion of the Overthrust Belt. (The Swans and Missions to the west are slabs which slope to the east. The slabs to the east in the Rocky Mountain Front slope to the west. Slabs in the Flathead Range slope both ways and are often piled in tiers like a wedding cake. From Silvertip Mountain through the White River

Great Northern Mountain. Left: The southwest face, showing the two spurs most commonly used to climb the peak. Right: The northeast side, showing Stanton Glacier

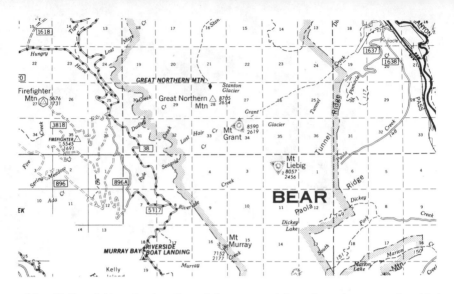

and the Flathead Alps, the junction of these two slab regimes is very noticeable.) Limestone and shale formed at the bottom of ancient seas. The Chinese Wall is limestone. Ripple marks are common in the Grinnell argillite, a red shale formation nearly 2000' thick.

Access: Between Lincoln and Glacier National Park. Only trails serve the mountainous areas. Major jumping-off points are in the Spotted Bear area above Hungry Horse Reservoir (from Highway 2) and at the Benchmark Trailhead (reached from Highway 287 at Augusta).

Ownership: Flathead, Lolo, Lewis and Clark, and Helena national forests.

THE GREAT BEAR AREA

Desert Mountain 6436 [D] Old lookout site.

Ousel Peak 7157 [W] Ridgetop trail to old lookout site. Easy way to get a great view of Glacier National Park.

Mt. Penrose 7875 [S] Gain the south ridge from the Highline Loop Road.

Firefighter Mountain 5676 [D] Manned lookout.

■ **Great Northern Mountain 8705** [S] Register. Take the East Side Road #38, which leaves Highway 2 as the main street of Martin City. Drive eight miles to Emery Creek and continue another 8½ miles, then turn left (uphill) and go ½ mile to the Highline Loop Road junction. Park at the bridge and start up through the brush south of the creek, angling to the right as you climb to get onto the south side of the ridge and out of the brush and huckleberries. Once on the ridgetop, follow it upward a mile, drop into a small timbered saddle, then go up the spur which ascends to the summit ridge north of the peak. This spur has clumps of gnarled trees up most of its length. Then follow goat trails and ledges up the summit ridge. The descent can be made down the open spur of loose scree which tops out right at the summit. There are one or two other western approaches to this popular peak on other long ridges that run to the summit ridge from the west. An eastern approach up Stanton Creek usually includes glacier travel, so take rope and ice axes there.

The southeast side of Kevan Mountain overlooks Lake Lavale. —U.S. Forest Service

Silvertip Mountain from its northeast ridge

East side of Three Sisters from the head of Baldy
Bear Creek
U.S. Forest Service

Mt. Grant 8590 [S] West ridge.

Mt. Liebig 8057 [S] South ridge from the saddle at the head of Paola Creek. This peak forms the southeast end of the Grant Ridge complex.

Felix Peak 7996 [S] Try the broken northeast ridge.

Red Sky Mountain 8173 [S] Northwest ridge.

Mt. Baptiste 8396 [S] Northwest ridge from saddle, or southwest ridge from Baptiste Lookout, 6698'.

Prospector Mountain 8105 [S] Approach from the east, or bushwhack up the southwest ridge.

Circus Peak 7829 [S]

Horseshoe Peak 7774 [S] North ridge. An old foot trail from Bradley Lake may be located.

Capitol Mountain 7868 [W]

Whitcomb Peak 7306 [S] Short scramble from trail.

Gunsight Rock 6998 [S] The center pillar is technical.

Gunsight Peak 7180 [W] Old lookout site.

Argosy Mountain 8155 [S]

THE BOB MARSHALL AREA

Spotted Bear Mountain 7276 [W] Actual summit ¼ mile southeast of the manned lookout at 7230'. A lookout has been there since 1914.

Trilobite Peak 8257 [S] You may encounter a little C-rated climbing up from the trail to the east.

Pentagon Mountain 8877 [S]

Kevan Mountain 8412 [S] Leave the trail at 8000'. Follow the south ridge ½ mile.

Point 8780 [S] North ridge from trail. This peak is a mile south of Kevan Mountain.

Hahn Peak 8310 [S] East approach.

Silvertip Mountain 8890 [S] This peak is flanked by a sprawling complex of ridges. The northeast ridge route begins at the saddle just south of Ibex Mountain, where you traverse under the east side of a little peak west of the saddle to gain the ridgetop. Once above timberline, traverse on the right side of two ridgetop knobs. Then the ridge turns westward to the peak, and you can dodge more lumps in the ridge on the south side. Another approach is a direct ascent just east of the north ridge. Expect moderately steep snow on this route.

There are two things to watch for if approaching up Silvertip Creek. A hunter trail heads east at the creek crossing just south of the hunting camp. This isn't the trail to Wall Creek, which is two miles upstream. Stay on the trail along the creek. Also, the 1975 and 1976 Forest Service maps show a trail loop from the north reaching almost to the peak. The entire loop does not exist, never has, never will. Use the 1982 Flathead National Forest map.

Lone Butte 8483 [S] Southeast side.

The Chinese Wall. The head of Moose Creek is in the foreground, where a low spot in the wall can be climbed without technical assistance. —U.S. Forest Service

A fire patrolman enjoys the view from the northwest ridge of Shale Peak (right) on July 16, 1927. Junction Mountain is in the distance (left), with the Flathead Alps in the middle distance. —U.S. Forest Service

Bungalow Mountain 8140 [W] Old lookout site.

Three Sisters 8900 [S] A line of three peaks on the same ridge. The northern peak is the highest, with the middle one 8630', and the southern one 8660'. All can be ascended by bushwhacking through alpine timber on the west side.

Redhead Peak 8798 [S] West side from Spotted Bear Pass.

Pagoda Mountain 8047 [S] Old lookout site. South ridge from nearby trail. Older trails may still be traceable to the top.

Mud Lake Mountain 6361 [W] Old lookout site.

Cliff Mountain 8576 [S] The high point of the Chinese Wall formation. Points atop the wall are most easily approached from the west.

Sphinx Peak 8540 [S] From the west, or from Haystack Mountain.

Slategoat Mountain 8887 [S] A huge complex of bare ridges and cliffs. Approach from any direction. Be prepared to make detours and explore. One possibility is the northeast ridge. Another is from the North Fork of Glenn Creek.

Sheep Mountain 8031 [S]

Haystack Mountain 8396 [W] Old lookout site.

Prairie Reef 8868 [W] Old lookout site.

Shale Peak 8080 [W]

Flathead Alps 8360 [S] A concentration of half a dozen peaks.

Junction Mountain 8700 [S] From the west.

Scintilla Mountain 8226 [S] Timbered top.

Twin Peaks 8744 [S] The south peak is 8719'.

THE SCAPEGOAT AREA

Scarlet Mountain 8164 [S] East side.

Patrol Mountain 8031 [W] Manned lookout.

The west side of Twin Peaks from Pearl Basin —U.S. Forest Service

The north side of Sugarloaf Mountain —U.S. Forest Service

Scapegoat Mountain from the north. Head of the Green Fork, lower right. Summit just above snowbank to the left. Evans Peak right of the summit, center of photo —U.S. Forest Service

Sugarloaf Mountain 8698 [S] Southeast face. The ridge from Observation Pass is more difficult.

Observation Point 8523 [W]

Flint Mountain 9079 [S] Southeast ramp.

Scapegoat Mountain 9204 [S] A little peak atop a massively buttressed plateau three miles across. The normal approach is from the northwest. From the head of the Green Fork it is a simple matter to get onto the summit plateau. The plateau can also be climbed from the south, or from the Cabin Creek-Dobrata Creek Divide where the trail goes to 8000'. The entire east side of the plateau is a line of cliffs. One break up through them is just south of the peak, where the east-facing line of cliffs makes a right-angle turn to the east. Scramble up the left-hand gully. At one spot, friction-climb a ten-foot high rounded cliff on the right (west) side of the drainage course.

You can also climb inside the mountain in extensive caves on the southeast cliffs.

Evans Peak 8979 [S] Northwest ridge, or use primitive trails approaching from the east.

Falls Point 7561 [W] Old lookout tower.

Olson Peak 8881 [S] Old lookout site. Old trails may help.

Crow Point 8611 [W]

Bugle Mountain 8171 [W]

Echo Mountain 8456 [S] Northeast or southeast ridge.

Red Mountain as seen from the east. The peak on the left is a satellite peak. —Bill Cunningham

Gunsight Rock, east of Spotted Bear Ranger Station —Kalispell Weekly News

127

Daly Peak 8313 [S] South ridge.

Arrastra Mountain 7976 [S] From the north. Old lookout site.

Red Mountain 9411 [W] A long approach by trail. To shorten the climb, park at the locked gate on the old logging road up Red Creek. The gate is on the north side of Copper Creek. From the end of the road, scramble up the right (north) side of the valley to gain the wonderful east ridge. There used to be a lookout tower on the summit. An alternate route, easy to find on the descent, drops eastward off the south ridge of Red Mountain to the little lake at the head of Red Creek.

Technical Opportunities: Close to home, there are small waterfalls along Highway 2 on Skiumah and Rescue creeks that ice up well. Gunsight Rock is only a two-hour drive on forest roads plus two more hours to get up the hill. There isn't much danger of finding this formation crowded with climbers, but you could experience the complete disappointment of finding the rock has toppled over if you put off your attempt too long. As for the wilderness areas, yes, you can climb cliffs in the Bob. You'll see some striking fragment of the earth's crust any place you look. Routes rate from moderately difficult to completely impossible. All the rock is shale, limestone, and related rotten brands.

Typical portion of the Chinese Wall, a formation nearly ten miles long —U.S. Forest Service

The Rocky Mountain Front in winter. Haystack Butte on the left —Ann Felstead

The Rocky Mountain Front

"Something of marvel must there be in a country which presents to the eye a succession of bewildering contrasts; where grandeur alternates with sadness; where the scarp of precipitous mountains frowns over an unending plains."
—George N. Curzon

Description: Ramparts of jagged, evenly-spaced north-south running ridges stand 5600' above the prairie. Lonely buttes lie to the east.

Geology: The Overthrust Belt piled up dramatically and evenly like a washboard, with a series of north-south valleys between the edges of limestone and argillite slabs. The limestone, only 300 million years old, makes up mountains directly overlooking the prairie, such as Castle Reef and Sawtooth Ridge. The large buttes on the plains (including Haystack Butte) are laccoliths (small batholiths), and the smaller adjacent formations are of related igneous and volcanic origin.

Access: West of Great Falls. County roads from the east end in the foothills, where trails head for all major drainages and some ridgetops. Popular approach routes include Gibson Reservoir Road #208 and Benchmark Road #235 from Augusta (Highway 287), and Teton River Road from Highway 89 five miles north of Choteau.

Ownership: Helena and Lewis and Clark national forests, Butte District Bureau of Land Management. Most of the outlying buttes are privately owned.

Choteau Mountain (left) swells out of the prairie north of the Teton River.

The north ridge of Rocky Mountain from Headquarters Pass —U.S. Forest Service

Crossing an ice gully high on the west side of Rocky Mountain —Randy Sandin

Ear Mountain overlooks prairie west of Choteau.

THE OVERTHRUST BELT

Mt. Baldy 7700 [J]

Forster Mountain 7872 [W] South ridge from end of the trail at 7736'.

Red Plume Mountain 7947 [W] Old lookout site.

Bullshoe Mountain 8006 [S]

Goat Mountain 8191 [S]

Half Dome Crag 8095 [W] Old lookout site.

Morningstar Mountain 8376 [S]

Mt. Field 8590 [S]

Mt. Drewyer 8236 [S]

Mt. Patrick Gass 8625 [S] South ridge.

Old Man of the Hills 8225 [S] West approach. East side approaches harder than a simple scramble.

Mt. Frazier 8327 [S] Southwest face.

Point 8602 [S] This unnamed peak is 2½ miles north of Mt. Wright, and north of Bruce Creek.

Mt. Wright 8875 [W] Old lookout site.

Choteau Mountain 8398 [S] North or south ridge.

Mt. Lockhart 8691 [S] Gain the south ridge from the west.

Teton Peak 8416 [S] From the northeast.

Old Baldy 9156 [S] Take a gully from Route Creek Pass to attain and ascend the north ridge. The peak can also be reached from Our Lake, an up-and-down route.

Beartop Point 8094 [W] Maintained lookout building.

Rocky Mountain 9392 [S] Three routes on the north side of this peak. The easy way is to leave the trail southwest of Headquarters Pass and go to the saddle west of the peak, then up the west face. Another way is to climb the jagged north ridge. Half way up you may want to traverse

Steamboat Point, with duck marsh to the northeast

East face of Sawtooth Ridge

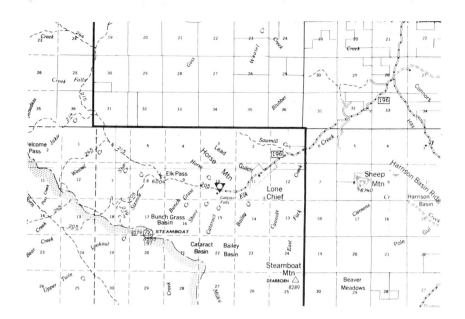

onto the west side to bypass an outcrop on the ridge. The upper part of the ridge is knife-edged and slightly exposed. You shouldn't need a rope in summer, but crouch to keep your balance if it's windy. A good descent route is the long scree slope on the peak's northeast flank. Run down this unusually large scree deposit, losing 1000' in ten minutes. Quick descents from sudden storms are never a problem on this mountain.

Ear Mountain 8580 [S] Northwest ridge, or other western approach.

Arsenic Peak 8498 [S] Northwest ridge. Other approaches about as easy.

Castle Reef 8330 [S] From the west. The most interesting way is up Hannon Gulch to where the creek makes a big dog-leg, ½ mile past the end of the road. Climb the north ridge from there. Descend the south ridge.

Sawtooth Ridge 8179 [S] Southwest slope from trail. The four peaks, all over 8000', can also be approached from the northwest.

Renshaw Mountain 8264 [S] Northwest ridge.

Fairview Mountain 8246 [S] South ridge, or climb the south ridge of the peak west of Fairview and then head east, dropping into the saddle and going up Fairview's west face.

Crown Mountain 8401 [S] From the south.

■ **Steamboat Point 8579** [W] Take Road #196, the Elk Creek Road, also the southern continuation of Augusta's main street. Watch for a road junction about ten miles out, just south of Haystack Butte, where you turn right. Go eight more miles to the end of the road. Park at the Elk Creek trailhead and walk two miles to Elk Pass. Locate the left fork of the trail, #205, and go another two miles. Then watch for Trail #239, which goes straight up the hill. Follow it the final steep three miles. At the top is an old lookout building, still manned during fire season.

Steamboat Mountain 8297 [S] From the south. For those who seek out exhausting, intricate routes. Takes all day.

Caribou Peak 8773 [S] South or west ridge from trail. Old lookout site.

Silver King Mountain 7771 [W] Manned lookout.

Haystack Butte. Steamboat Mountain to the south is also visible. —Randy Sandin ·

Square Butte

East side of Electric Mountain

Coburn Mountain (left) and adjacent butte

THE OUTLYING BUTTES

Pine Butte 5012 [S] A low, picturesque butte covered with limber pine. Grizzly bears from the wilderness use the brushy swamp to the west for feeding, bedding, and breeding.

Haystack Butte 6821 [S] From the northwest. Circle around to the west near the top to avoid obstructions.

Crown Butte 4710 [S] South or west side. This laccolith is four miles south of Simms. Cliffs of its exposed igneous core defend the top, unattainable to livestock and covered by undisturbed native grasses. The Nature Conservancy, owner of the butte, suggests no fires, dogs, or camping. Watch for rattlesnakes.

Shaw Butte 4643 [J] Two miles east of Simms.

Square Butte 4793 [W] Old jeep trail on the south side. The top is large (about two square miles) and still has stands of tall native grasses. A homesteader tried to make a go of it on this butte in the 1920s, but couldn't establish an adequate water supply. In 1960 a local rancher brought up water from springs at the butte's base and began limited summer grazing.

Point 4932 [S] Prairie hill seven miles northeast of Bowmans Corners. Road to radio facilities on the west side.

Point 5398 [S] South ridge. Just north of Sullivan Hill.

West side of The Reef

Sullivan Hill 5485 [J] Drive up the southeast side, or scramble up the grassy west ridge.

Center Point 5031 [S] Two miles south of Bowmans Corners.

Lionhead Butte 5063 [S] From the southeast. Note: Lionhead, Birdtail, Haystack, and Fishbank buttes are all reached by private access—get permission first.

Birdtail Butte 5028 [C] From the west. Steep near the top.

Haystack Butte 4978 [S] From the southwest.

Fishbank Butte 4916 [S] West approach.

Sullivan Point 5259 [S] South shoulder. Old lookout site.

Skull Butte 5687 [S] The eastern point of a pair of buttes, Black Butte (5442') to the west. Both reached from the saddle in between.

Mt. Cecelia 6142 [S] Southwest shoulder. Timbered summit.

Antelope Butte 5215 [S]

Finigan Mountain 5462 [S] Timber-topped butte five miles west of Cascade.

Electric Mountain 5312 [S] Closest approach from the southeast. Its satellite peak ½ mile northeast is 5382'. The Reef, two long ridges of upthrust rock, comes together at Electric Mountain and continues southward as one ridge.

Coburn Mountain 5189 [S]

Technical Opportunities: The entire Overthrust Belt has exposed limestone, with colossal cliffs in the central portion. There are limestone spires in the Antelope Butte area west of Bynum Reservoir. In the outlying buttes, cliffs and dikes are composed of a dark crystalline igneous rock called shonkinite, usually occurring in vertical columns or palisades. It is fairly hard—certainly more reliable than the limestone to the west. On large buttes, the shonkinite forms a continuous series of arêtes.

Dearborn River south of Augusta. The limestone cliffs are typical of the scenic but low-quality climbing in the Overthrust Belt.

Nevada Valley north of Avon

Looking west from Union Peak —U.S. Forest Service

North side Hoodoo Mountain

The Garnet Range

"Climb the mountains and get their good tidings.
Nature's peace will flow into you, as sunshine flows into trees.
The winds will blow their own freshness into you, and the storms their energy,
While cares will drop off like autumn leaves."

—John Muir

Description: Low profile groups of broad forested hills and ridgetops, with meadows and open timber up high. Elevation span 4800'.

Geology: The Garnets themselves are sedimentary layers bulldozed by movement of the Sapphire Block. The satellite range to the east, between Helena and Lincoln, was not disturbed by the block, and contains granitic intrusions and volcanic extrusives.

Access: Between Missoula and Helena. Highways, forest roads, jeep and foot trails serve the entire area. The Garnet Range Road leaves Highway 200 five miles east of Potomac.

Ownership: Helena National Forest, Butte District Bureau of Land Management.

WEST OF HIGHWAY 141

Bonner Mountain 6813 [W] Jeep trail to radio facilities on the west ridge, 5985'. Timbered summit.

Union Peak 6810 [P] Manned lookout. Road passable for cars.

Mt. Baldy 6941 [S] South face.

Granite Mountain 6898 [S] Southwest ridge. Timbered top.

Chamberlain Mountain 6860 [S] West approach. Timbered top.

Elevation Mountain 7073 [J] Walk ¼ mile from jeep trail to top.

Saddle Mountain 7004 [S] Northwest ridge from jeep trail at old lookout site, 6814'.

Hoodoo Mountain 7210 [S] Flat timbered top.

Mitchell Mountain (left) from the southeast

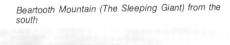

Beartooth Mountain (The Sleeping Giant) from the south

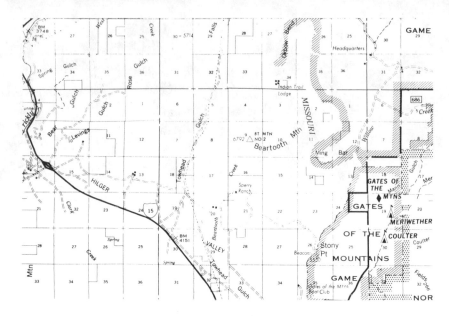

Devil Mountain 7438 [S] Southeast ridge (Fourth of July Ridge) from trail. Top mostly timbered.

Old Baldy Mountain 7511 [S] Northeast ridge from nearby jeep trail.

Colt Point 6982 [W] Trail crosses Mannix Park.

EAST OF HIGHWAY 141

Ogden Mountain 7405 [S] Southeast ridge from Trail #404. Timbered summit.

Dalton Mountain 6767 [D] Old lookout site.

Fields Point 7428 [S] Nearby trail on the west side. This point, not shown on the Forest Service map, is about three miles east of Dalton Mountain.

Crater Mountain 7128 [W] Jeep trail ¼ mile east.

Granite Butte 7600 [D] Old lookout site.

Lyon Point 7738 [J] The Sawmill Gulch jeep trail may no longer be passable to the top. Access across private land.

Mitchell Mountain 7031 [J] Access across private land.

■ **Beartooth Mountain 6792** [S] Leave Interstate 15 at the Gates of the Mountains interchange 17 miles north of Helena, or the Sieben interchange seven miles farther, and use the map shown to drive up Beartooth Creek. Access is across private land, so watch for posted instructions. Park near the Sperry Ranch, or in Section 18 in Towhead Gulch, and head up the southwest shoulder of the mountain to gain the west ridge. Stroll to the top. This mountain is also known as The Sleeping Giant because of its appearance from the Helena area. Once on top, you'll be standing on the giant's chest. The giant's nose, 6053', can be scrambled up the north side. Technical opportunities on it are limited due to loose rock. The nose used to be one of two twin tusks, which is how Beartooth Mountain got its name. The 500' eastern tooth was described by Lewis and Clark. In 1878 the spire dislodged and crashed down, sliding as rubble for ¼ mile,

Mt. Belmont, sagebrush hills to the east   *Scratchgravel Hills, from Helena's north side*

leveling the forest as it went. Hunters miles away heard a roar and felt the earth shake. (With the coming of the white man, nature tore down the Bear Tooth and put a sleeping man in its place. Let's hope Montana's remaining Beartooth Spire, south of Red Lodge, will continue to stand.)

Nevada Mountain 8293 [S] Short scramble up the south side from trail.

Black Mountain 8338 [W] Trail to the east. Timbered top.

Meyers Hill 7132 [J] A flat, grassy knob. A car can get within ¼ mile on the south side.

Mt. Belmont 7330 [D] A ski lift climbs the east side.

Scratchgravel Point 5253 [W] Head up the south ridge of the higher eastern hill.

Technical Opportunities: Most of the range has no exposed rock. Sometimes small broken cliffs of lousy rock can be found along the watercourses. The best climbing is in Blue Cloud Spires just west of Helena. Granite boulders and pinnacles are scattered through timber and scrubland in Blue Cloud and Sweeney creeks. These outcrops mark the northern limit of the Boulder Batholith. Some access is across private land.

Spires above Sweeney Creek

Stacked boulders poke out of timber between Blue Cloud and Sweeney creeks.

Northwest side of Table Mountain

Mt. Helena overlooks its namesake.

North side of Red Mountain under the first snow of late summer

The Boulder Batholith Area

"Because it's there, and we're mad."

—Warren "Batso" Harding

Description: A dome-shaped upland, with a few major peaks in the Highland Mountains, elevation span 5900'. Elsewhere scrubby timber is interspersed with boulder outcrops.

Geology: The Boulder Batholith formed 72 million years ago. Volcanic activity deposited brown and green rocks on the granitic underlayment. Erosion and weathering removed the top layers, exposing extensive boulder fields already formed by chemical decomposition. These outcrops are usually on south exposures, where soil would easily dry and blow off. Rock in the southern Highlands is metamorphic and about three billion years old. Granites and sedimentary rocks like gneiss are common, with marble in places.

Access: Around Butte. Interstate 15 and other highways get close to most objectives. Back roads and trails are common, but cross-country travel is necessary to the more rugged places.

Ownership: Helena and Deerlodge national forests, Butte District Bureau of Land Management.

Gentle slopes, west side of the Boulder Batholith

The Three Brothers dominate southwest of Helena.

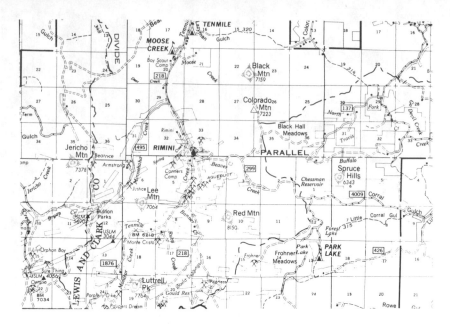

NORTHWEST OF INTERSTATE 15

Mt. Helena 5460 [W] Helena's backyard mountain. The trail starts on Adams Street on the west side of downtown Helena (actually the highest part of town).

Colorado Mountain 7223 [J] Old lookout site.

■ **Red Mountain 8150** [S] Turn south off Highway 12 nine miles west of Helena and drive the Tenmile Creek Road seven miles to the old mining town of Rimini. Continue 3½ miles past Rimini, and park ¼ mile past a water ditch where the road makes a sharp right. Just behind you the trail, an old mining road, takes off on the left side of the road. The trail goes about ½ mile up a stream, then turns right (south). At this point head straight up the hill (northeast), scrambling through a rock slide to a saddle on the south ridge of Red Mountain. Stroll to the top.

Sugarloaf Mountain 8263 [S] Short scramble from nearby trail.

Cliff Mountain 8381 [S] Short scramble from nearby trails.

Thunderbolt Mountain 8597 [W] Old lookout site.

Bison Mountain 8028 [S] North or south ridge from jeep trail.

Three Brothers 8565 [S] From the northwest. Three partially timbered summits. North summit 8480', south one 8512', middle summit highest.

Jack Mountain 8739 [P] Old lookout building.

Mt. Thompson 7925 [S] Short scramble from jeep road.

Pole Mountain 7599 [S]

Gospel Hill 7346 [S] From the south. Timbered summit.

Blizzard Hill 7658 [J] Old lookout site.

Cotton Point 7243 [S] Southeast shoulder.

Sheepshead Mountain 7780 [W]

Rampart Mountain 7768 [S] Overlooks Butte. Climb East Ridge Point from the east.

South side of McClusky Mountain

Bull Mountain from the north

Highland Lookout. Butte in the distance

Switchbacks in the Highland Lookout Road

SOUTHEAST OF INTERSTATE 15

Haystack Mountain 8821 [W]

Maxwell Point 8251 [D] Television facilities. Also called X-L Heights. Overlooks Butte. Technical rock routes near the TV towers.

McClusky Mountain 8121 [S] Timbered summit. Traverse off the south side near the top, or continue up the technical rock face.

Bull Mountain 8609 [S] Register. Southeast side from Big Chief Park.

Fitz Point 8141 [J] Grassy top.

SOUTH OF INTERSTATE 90

Mt. Humbug 8266 [J] Grassy top.

Lime Kiln Hill 8086 [J] Grassy top.

■ **Red Mountain 10070** [W] Drive south from Butte on Highway 10 to about seven miles past the airport. Take the Highland City-Blacktail Creek turnoff, a right-hand Y where the highway climbs out of the creek and into tight turns. In about ten miles take a left onto Road #8520, then another left in another mile onto Road #8514, the Highland Lookout Road. It's about 3½ miles to Highland Lookout, 9701'. This road is suitable for pickups. A car can make it, but take one you wouldn't mind abandoning. Park at the lookout and take the goat trail the final 370' up the north ridge. The lookout used to sit there, but was struck by lightning until blasted apart. The present structure, although in a more protected location, is the highest manned lookout in Montana.

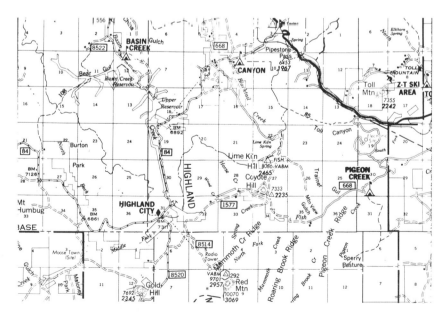

Thunderhead over Homestake Pass

Table Mountain (left) seen from the summit of Red Mountain

Table Mountain 10223 [S] Climb Red Mountain, then scramble on scree, goat trails, and boulder meadows up and down the connecting ridge.

Negro Mountain 8387 [J] Grassy top.

McCartney Mountain 8364 [S] Two-mile scramble up the southwest ridge. Timbered top. The east summit, 8216', reached by jeep trail. Better view from its grassy summit.

Bell Peak 7865 [S] South ridge.

Block Mountain 5995 [S] Southeast ridge. Other approaches quite steep.

The Hogback 6018 [S] Northwest side from mine road.

Technical Opportunities: In the Boulder Batholith, technical work is the primary climbing activity. The rock is crisp, hard, and geologically young. While the area is not massive and overwhelming like the Bitterroots or Beartooths, it does contain the highest quality technical granite in Montana. One is confronted by many challenging innuendos, including boulders not visible above the timber. Rattlesnakes sometimes inspire local climbers to new moves and techniques. Under less drastic conditions these climbers consider where bolts might be appropriate, such as on the thousands of blank-faced outcrops lurking about. The larger more popular spires with ample crack routes are kept free of permanent hardware in the interests of aesthetics.

Tenmile Creek: A boulder practice area is just south of Rimini.

Sheep Mountain: There are spire-like outcrops on the east side of this mountain a couple miles northwest of Clancy. One has a shaft in the middle of its summit. At the foot of Sheep Mountain are practice boulders.

Homestake Pass: Boulder fields extend from here northeast past Whitetail Reservoir to Boulder, and include spires, shark fins, and monoliths. There's a nice dome ¼ mile north of the pass. The Dragonsback, on the north side of the freeway five miles east of the pass, is interesting with one or two pitches of intermediate difficulty.

Looking northeast across the 100-acre summit of Table Mountain

Spire Rock, northeast of Homestake Pass

*Along the freeway east of
Homestake Pass:
Blank-faced slabs (left) and
The Dragonsback (right)*

Pipestone Pass: There is one dominant formation, Our Rock, on the south side of the highway just east of the pass. Routes were pioneered up its 150' north face with pitons, but chocks and other modern hardware will prove useful. Your layback, stemming, jamming, and chimneying skills will get a workout. Hand holds are limited in spots where you'll rely on friction holds. Depending on the route, you may want some direct aid near the top. On the back side of the tower are short practice pitches that can be top-roped and rappelled.

Humbug Spires: Southwest of Butte. This area contains practice boulders, gullies, chimneys, dihedrals, jam cracks, roofs, and blank faces. Short crag routes and bouldering problems from simple to hopeless beckon by the thousands. On large spires preferred routes go up vertical crack systems. Nine of these spires are 300' to 600' high, with another 50 shorter spires. The Wedge is the largest individual spire. The Crown, also prominent, overhangs on all sides. There are also outcrops all over the place northeast of the main concentration of spires, west of Basin Creek. While the quality of the rock is really swell, watch for scattered little pockets of obvious white granite which is very scaly and not reliable for friction holds.

*Our Rock, in Pipestone
Pass*

A dihedral in the Humbug Spires

The main group of spires is reached by hiking up Moose Creek, then turning right up a timbered gulch at a small old barn. The Bureau of Land Management closes the Moose Creek Road sometimes in the spring. Approaches can also be made up Lime Gulch or from the Tucker River area, but contact the landowner first.

Views of Humbug Spires

Elkhorn Peak from the north

The Elkhorn Mountains

"This hilltop is your place, your beloved place; all that is around you is under your care. You must look after everything here and everything will in turn look after you."
—Carlos Castaneda

Description: A small, timbered, relatively featureless range of high meadows and broad ridges, with prominent boulder-covered peaks spanning 5600' in the southern portion. The grassy upland south of the main Elkhorn group has scattered prominent points.

Geology: Recent volcanic activity. Eastern part underlain by folded sediments, western part on the eastern edge of the Boulder Batholith.

Access: Southeast of Helena. Dirt roads from perimeter highways (mostly #287) serve trails to the central uplands.

Ownership: Helena and Deerlodge national forests, Butte District Bureau of Land Management.

Spokane Point 5518 [P] Aircraft beacon. The Spokane Hills are northwest of Winston.

Shingle Butte 5930 [S] Southeast approach.

Strawberry Butte 6168 [P] Manned lookout.

Casey Peak 8499 [W] A trail (not shown on the new Forest Service map) starts from Casey Meadows and goes up the northwest ridge. Old lookout remains on the summit.

High Peak 8534 [S] Leave trail and head through timber on the southeast shoulder.

Crazy Point 8770 [S] Climb through timber on the west side from Trail #115, or head up the southeast ridge from Trail #138.

View from McClellan Creek of Casey Peak   *Close-up view of Casey Peak*   145

Elkhorn Peak from the summit of Crow Peak

Goat hunters rest on Crow Peak. Tizer Basin to the north

Point 8777 [S] Two miles southeast of Crazy Point. Take the northwest ridge from Trail #138, or come in from a mining road in Indian Creek which ends on the east ridge.

Elkhorn Peak 9381 [S] Register. West ridge, reached by jeep trail from the old mining town of Elkhorn.

■ **Crow Peak 9414** [S] Turn northeast off Highway 69 about six miles southeast of Boulder. Follow signs for 13 miles to the ghost town of Elkhorn. At the north end of town, look for the road that climbs onto the hill east of town and follow it a little over a mile to Queen Gulch. Or take the Queen Gulch Road two miles south of Elkhorn. Either way it's about six miles of four-wheel-drive mining road to the Elkhorn Skyline Mine. Park near where the road begins to descend to the mine and look for the unmarked trail, #131. If you can't find it, it's still easy going to the east ridge of Crow Peak. Finish your jaunt up this ridge and look for the register box. This peak can also be reached from Elkhorn Peak on the connecting ridge.

Lone Mountain 5024 [S] Isolated grassy hill. Five miles south of Radersburg.

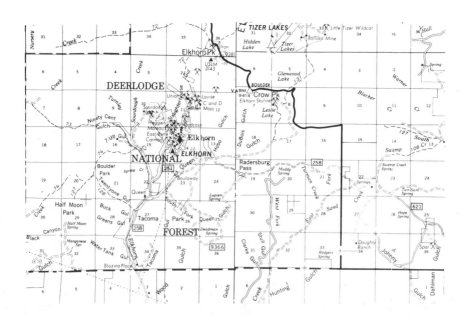

Boulder stack in the forest understory, McClellan Creek

High Peak 5610 [S] Eight miles south of Toston. A jeep road over grassy hills gets within ½ mile on the southwest side.

Doherty Mountain 6400 [S] South ridge. Four miles northeast of Cardwell.

London Point 6326 [S] Patriarch of the London Hills, two miles southwest of Lewis and Clark Caverns. Attain the south ridge from the southwest.

Technical Opportunities: Outlying granite outcrops of the Boulder Batholith can be found up McClellan Creek and on slopes east of Muskrat Creek near Boulder. These formations consist of boulders scattered through the woods, and an occasional small spire.

Towering cumulus clouds consolidate into a thunderstorm over the Tobacco Roots. Notice the extensive alluvial fans on the west side of this range.

View from Mt. Jefferson of western Tobacco Roots, from Old Baldy Mountain (far right) to Granite Peak (left center)

Northeast aspect of Granite Peak. Note old prospect roads. Cloudrest Peak on right skyline

The Tobacco Root Mountains

"I want to solve a mountaineering problem in the mountains and not in a sporting goods store."

—Reinhold Messner

Description: A compact plateau with concentrated peaks of the same general elevation. Loose fractured rock from top to bottom. Elevation span 6400'.

Geology: A heavily glaciated 50-million-year-old granitic core surrounded by basement metamorphics, the first generation of rock on the planet.

Access: Southeast of Butte, and set back from paved highways. Mill Creek Road #111 from Highway 287 at Sheridan is a good route into the central core of the peaks. Trails and mining roads serve most of the range.

Ownership: Deerlodge and Beaverhead national forests.

Background: By pristine standards this range is all torn up, bearing the scars of extensive mining. Most claims and roads are not the environmental degradation of corporate exploiters, but the activity of daring prospectors who many years ago eked out a living from a most adverse and brutal landscape. Appreciate the small marks they have left on these mighty and destitute remnants of ancient geological holocausts.

Manhead Mountain 9966 [S] Register. East side from McGovern Creek.

Point 10574 [S] From Brannan Lakes. Unnamed peak, third-highest in the range.

Lakeshore Mountain 10457 [S] Southeast ridge from Crystal Lake.

Apa Mountain 10400 [S] Southwest ridge from Low Pass.

Mt. Jackson 10424 [S] Northwest ridge from Crystal Lake.

Old Baldy Mountain 9901 [S] Southeast ridge from Leiterville, or north ridge from Independence Gulch Pass.

Southeast face of Hollowtop Mountain from Mt. Jefferson

High school students on a church outing sign the register on Hollowtop Mountain.

Branham Peak and Upper Branham Lake

Leggat Spire, actually the end of the east ridge of Leggat Peak

Sunrise Peak 10195 [S] East face from Sunrise Lake.

Spuhler Peak 10421 [S] North side from Sunrise Lake.

Hollowtop Mountain 10604 [S] Register. From Upper Cataract Creek there's a jeep trail to Lower Mason Lake. From there come up the hollowed out gully. Then get on the northeast rim of the mountain and follow it to the top. This summit can also be reached by the south ridge from the Nicholson Mine, or by technical broken granite faces on the east side. Note: This peak is identified as Mt. Jefferson on older USFS and USGS maps. A look at the mountain from Three Forks shows the obvious hollow top.

Mt. Jefferson 10513 [S] From Hollowtop Lake, or the southwest side from the Nicholson Mine. This mine is still active, so sometimes the jeep road is closed for safety reasons. (The road is too rocky and steep for ore trucks to stop immediately when loaded.) You can still hike or take a motorbike to the 9000' base of operations. Note: Mt. Jefferson is identified as Hollowtop Mountain on many old maps.

Middle Mountain 10353 [S] Register. Northeast ridge via a saddle south of Louise Lake, or a C-rated route from the same lake.

Horse Mountain 10222 [S] From the southeast or the Nicholson Mine.

Potosi Peak 10125 [S] North ridge from Albro Lake.

Noble Peak 10396 [C] Either the south ridge from Noble Lake or the northeast ridge from Lost Cabin Lake. The actual summit is teepee-shaped and has a technical route on its north side.

Granite Peak 10590 [S] Northeast shoulder from old mining road, or the southeast side from Granite Lake.

Cloudrest Peak 10087 [S] North face from Blossom Lake.

Lonesome Peak 10401 [S] Southeast side.

Thompson Peak 10382 [S] Go northeast from Thompson Reservoir to gain the flat east ridge.

Leggat Peak 10216 [S] Gain the west ridge from the South Fork of Indian Creek.

Revenue Flats west of Norris

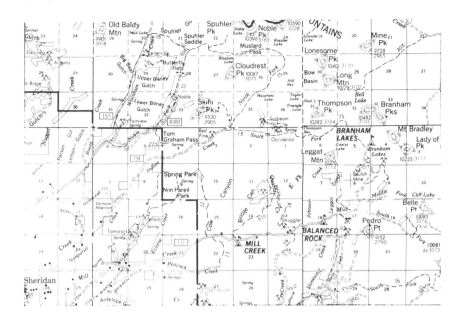

■ **Branham Peak 10482** [S] Drive east up the Mill Creek Road from Sheridan (car road) 15 miles to the Branham Lakes Campground. From the north end of the upper lake head northwest up a broad gully to a saddle in the west ridge of the peak, then up that ridge.

Belle Point 10085 [S] South of the west ridge from the South Fork of Mill Creek, then up the west ridge.

Ward Peak 10267 [S] Southwest ridge from mine, or other south side approaches.

Porphyry Mountain 10081 [S] East ridge from mine.

Ramshorn Mountain 10201 [S] North ridge from Porphyry Mountain.

Point 10243 [S] Unnamed peak east of Porphyry Mountain. Mine on its northeast side at 10000'.

South Baldy Mountain 10109 [W] Old trail.

Technical Opportunities: Revenue Flats (near the old Revenue Mine) has scattered spires of a dark, abrasive granite, and is a fine practice area. More involved climbs can be made up the South Boulder River, where there are some moderate-sized formations (2-3 pitches), with many smaller ones skulking about in the trees. West of Branham Lake, on the east side of Leggat Peak, is a dark solid metamorphic face topping out at 10089', for some rock work at altitude. Another sheer prow tops out on the north ridge of Manhead Mountain.

Medicine Man (right) and nearby granite outcrops west of Hollowtop Mountain on the Upper East Fork of the South Boulder River

The Centennials overlook high prairie and sagebrush.

Ruby Range—northeast side

Ashbough Point from Blue Mountain —Bureau of Land Management

The Ruby River Ranges

"The mountains lie in curves so tender
I want to lay my arm around them
As God does."

—Olive Tilford Dargan

Description: Scattered ranges on a 5000' upland. The Ruby Range is small, steep in spots, and covered with scrub timber. The Blacktails are mostly high grassy flats. The Snowcrests come in odd shapes and are mostly grassy, though high scree is common. The Gravellys are grassy on top, with timber in the draws, and a not-so-obvious elevation span of 5800'. The Centennials have long, grassy ridgetops over successive limestone escarpments alternating with steep slopes of loose rock and small trees.

Geology: All these uplifted fault blocks have exposed Precambrian basement rocks, including gneisses, schists, and granites. Marble (metamorphosed limestone) occurs along the west edge of the Ruby Range. The Blacktails have completely eroded down to the tops of their alluvial fans.

Access: East of Dillon. Ruby River Road #100 south from Highway 287 at Alder connects with Gravelly Range Road #347 and with Snowcrest Range trailheads. The Centennials are reached from the Centennial Valley Road, which leaves Interstate 15 at Monida.

Ownership: Beaverhead National Forest, Butte District Bureau of Land Management, U.S. Sheep Experiment Station.

THE RUBY RANGE

Ruby Point 9391 [W] A jeep road and pack trail from the south, and a trail most of the way up Laurin Creek.

East side, Sliderock Mountain

Blue Mountain from Ashbough Point —Bureau of Land Management

Hogback Mountain from the east

East side of Olson Peak

THE BLACKTAIL MOUNTAINS

Gallagher Mountain 8477 [S] East side from primitive road.

Ashbough Point 9173 [S] Grassy top. The northeast ridge is direct. The long south ridge is open and flat. Blue Mountain, a flat-topped sister summit, lies northwest.

Blacktail Mountain 9477 [W] On the south end of Ashbough Ridge, surrounded by large high grassy expanses. One can stroll from jeep trails west or east of Peak 9247.

Red Point 9240 [J] Radio facilities. Grass-topped, south of Gallagher Mountain. A completely eroded mountain. Not even a bloody stump remains. The summit is the top of the mountain's alluvial fan.

THE SNOWCREST RANGE

Sliderock Mountain 10439 [S] South ridge, gained from the east or west.

Hogback Mountain 10605 [S] Southwest ridge from The Notch.

Olson Peak 10486 [S] South ridge from mine.

Sunset Peak 10581 [S] North ridge from mine.

Stonehouse Mountain 10075 [W] High point of a seven-mile-long ridge which trails off to the south.

Sawtooth Mountain 10090 [S] West ridge.

Antone Peak 10247 [S] East ridge or northwest spur.

THE GRAVELLY RANGE

Baldy Mountain 9600 [S] North spur from the Garrison Mine, reached from Alder Gulch south of Virginia City.

Sheep Mountain 9697 [S] East ridge from Romy Lake. The ridges of this mountain are collectively called the Greenhorn Range.

Big Horn Mountain 10281 [S] West ridge from the Gravelly Range Road.

■ **Black Butte 10545** [S] A black mass of volcanic rock. The bones of prehistoric animals have been found on it. Indian legend says that somewhere within this mountain is an underground stream of clear water, with a pebbly bed half gravel and half gold nuggets. The stream flows in a cavern which once served as a pathway to a geyser vent. Geysers were common in the area not

The Snowcrest Trail follows the top of the long south ridge of Stonehouse Mountain.

Antone Peak's grassy south side

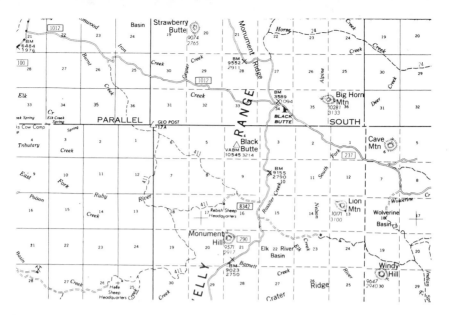

long ago. The legend goes on to say that the Indians carried away hundreds of pounds of nuggets each year to make into ornaments. Two chiefs quarreled over entrance rights to the sacred cavern. A great war resulted, and the stream ran red. Clouds darkened the land for three days, earth-quakes ripped through the region, and all the geysers dried up. When the sun came back out, the mountain's shape had changed from that of a crouching mountain lion into a giant armed with a club crouching over the treasure. Then the Great Spirit spoke through the mountain saying, "Whosoever tries to break into the sealed sacred treasure house shall perish without mercy or delay." Thus some centuries before Columbus made his voyage, this story was firmly entrenched in the lore of the western Indians.

In the 1500s along came the Spaniards looking for the Seven Golden Cities of Cibola, which lay somewhere north of Mexico. In 1836, according to Crow Indian legend, a party of "trappers" wearing Spanish dress made it to the area, looked around, and expressed interest in mining. There is nothing recorded of their fate, but the Spanish Peaks to the east are named for them. Whether or not the Gravelly Range is a rich gold deposit, it has an immense gravel deposit which, like a river bed, follows the top of the range. In the early 1860s poor bumbling prospectors, completely ignorant of the legend of the sacred cavern, blundered into all kinds of gold in the gulches heading up in this range. The towns of Alder Gulch and Virginia City were born at one of the richest placer diggings ever found on this planet. Afterwards, Black Butte remained isolated and seldom visited. An occasional horse thief was disposed of by vigilantes in the mountain's shadow. Later, sheep were brought up to summer pasture. In the 1940s a hunter is rumored to have tracked a black bear into a cave and seen the sacred river. Afterwards he heard the Indian legend and returned, but could not locate the entrance.

Today you can see Black Butte, a geyser basin, and a mountain range made of gravel. You, of course, are a practical climber and don't believe in irresponsible rumors and legends. Get on the Gravelly Range Road by either driving south up the Ruby River from Alder, or turn west off Highway 287 nine miles south of Ennis. A Forest Service brochure describes the Self-Guided

North side of Baldy Mountain

Sheep Mountain and the Greenhorn Range from the south   **155**

The Gravelly Range Road follows the broad crest of the range as high as 9552'. —U.S. Forest Service

East side of Black Butte —U.S. Forest Service

Range Tour of the Gravellys. The road is pretty bad when wet. Park east of Black Butte. It is impossible to get the butte confused with any other peak in the range. Walk up to it, ascend through a triangle of open timber, then scramble up the east side through loose rock to the top, where there is a register. At the summit sit down on top of all that gold and eat your heart out. Or look out and notice the beauty of this area and how good you feel. Greater treasure has no man.

Lion Mountain 10171 [S] Southeast ridge.

Antelope Peak 8280 [S] Southeast ridge from Brundage Creek. The high point of a two-mile-long prairie ridge at the south end of the range.

THE CENTENNIAL MOUNTAINS

Baldy Mountain 9889 [S] Take a P-rated road up a grass ramp on the south side of Tipton Creek. Park and follow the west ridge. From the top of the ridge head east, traversing under three points to get to the peak. A shorter approach can be made by bushwhacking from the north.

Sheep Mountain 9683 [S] Several routes. From the north gain the west ridge two miles from the summit, then traverse through grassy flats on the south side of the ridge. Another way is to bushwhack south from the road to take a gully directly up the west face. Or scramble up a steep gully on the northwest face. Expect a little C-rated terrain near the top. Finally, try from the saddle between Sheep and Taylor mountains.

Taylor Mountain 9855 [S] From the saddle between it and Sheep Mountain, or up a spur northeast of the peak (east of a cirque on the side of the mountain) to gain the east ridge. It's then westward 1½ miles to the top. There's a jeep road on the Idaho side.

Mt. Jefferson 10196 [S] Scramble up Cole Creek south of Red Rock Pass to the state line divide and follow the snaking ridgetop southward to the summit. This point is on the Continental Divide. But catch this: The Pacific side is to the east. Waters flowing to the Atlantic originate on the west side of this mountain.

Technical Opportunities: Well, not really. One might find something reasonably firm in the lower drainages. Higher formations are mostly limestone and volcanic debris. Outcrops in Red Rock Canyon aren't too good, either. One who likes to try different rock might give it a go, as some formations, especially in the Centennials, are unusual.

South side of Antelope Peak

Baldy Mountain

Sheep Mountain

Outcrops up Hell Roaring Creek in the Centennials

Taylor Mountain

Mt. Jefferson from above Red Rock Pass. The summit is the second peak from the left.

Thunderclouds in the Sweetgrass Hills

Wind blows across fields of wheat southwest of West Butte. Southwest spur plainly visible

Southeast side of Gold Butte

The North Prairie

"An' the prairie an' the butte-tops an' the long winds when they blow,
Is like the things what Adam knew on his birthday, long ago."

—Anonymous

Description: Massive isolated hills. The Bearpaws are timbered on the west, grassy on the east. The elevation span between Bearpaw Baldy and the Missouri River is 4000'. The Little Rockies have awesome thickets of scrubby timber surrounding openings of fractured rock. The Sweetgrass Hills have timber sandwiched between grassy tops and bases.

Geology: Most of the prairie is part of the Fort Union formation—sediments from a shallow sea and adjacent coastal plain (inhabited by dinosaurs) 60 to 70 million years ago. The buttes and small mountains are uplifts protruding through the formation. The Sweetgrass Hills are a cluster of 25-million-year-old granitic laccoliths. The Bearpaws are similar, but the rock is exotic igneous material, flanked north and south by volcanic extrusives. The Little Rockies are a dome of uplifted basement rocks surrounded by concentric circles of younger sedimentary rocks—a limestone ring is particularly visible. The Larb Hills are simply debris piled up by continental glaciers.

Access: North of Great Falls and the Missouri River. Highways and county roads go to all areas. Roads to the Sweetgrass Hills begin at Sunburst (on Interstate 15) and Chester (on Highway 2). Roads to the Bearpaws head south from Highway 2 at Havre and Chinook. The Little Rockies are best entered through Hays (Highway 66) or Zortman (Highway 191).

Ownership: Lewistown District Bureau of Land Management, Rocky Boy and Fort Belknap Indian reservations, private holdings.

Haystack Butte. Fields of corn are an unusual obstacle.

The west side of East Butte, showing Mt. Brown (left) and Mt. Royal (center)

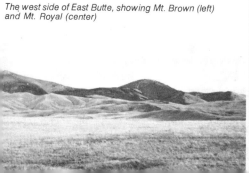

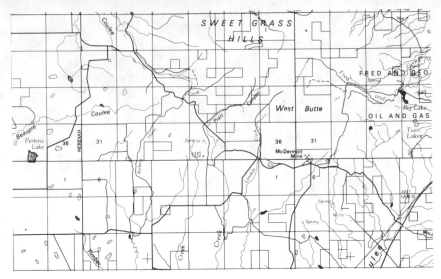

THE MARIAS RIVER AREA

Landslide Butte 4685 [D] Northwest of Cutbank. Gravel pit on it.

Chalk Butte 4308 [S]

Big Crown Butte 4662 [S] West of Cutbank.

Black Buttes 4410 [S] Five miles north of Pendroy.

Teton Ridge 4204 [W] Ten miles east of Choteau.

The Knees 3865 [D] Twin buttes 23 miles east of Brady. West Knee has a radio tower on its west end and stands 500' above the prairie. East Knee, S-rated, is 3695'.

Goose Bill Butte 3769 [P] Three miles off Highway 223, 18 miles out of Fort Benton, in Section 26 of Township 27 North, Range 7 East.

Floweree Butte 4036 [S] From the northwest.

THE SWEETGRASS HILLS

■ **West Butte 6983** [S] Turn off Interstate 15 at Sunburst and head east, staying on the main county road. This road turns north after 13 miles then skirts West Butte on its right (south) side. Park close to the butte near a fence and hike up the grassy southwest spur. Past the top of the spur an ascending animal trail angles left across rocky openings and on to the summit.

Gold Butte 6512 [S] Take the road west from Whitlash to the north side of the butte. The west side is also close to a road.

Grassy Butte 4429 [D] Radio facilities. Old lookout site.

Black Jack Butte 5201 [S] From the north.

Mt. Brown 6958 [S] The north end of East Butte. Head up the south ridge from a corral in the saddle, or try the north ridge.

Mt. Royal 6914 [J] Radio facilities. The south end of East Butte.

Mt. Lebanon 5807 [S] Southeast ridge.

Haystack Butte 4737 [S] Southwest slope.

Evening sun on wheat stubble as storm shreds disperse around Centennial Mountain

North side of Baldy Mountain

On a cow trail in a coulee, west side of Lloyd Butte

Murphy Butte from the northwest

THE BEARPAW MOUNTAINS

Saddle Butte 3143 [S] Two miles southeast of Havre. Scramble east ½ mile from the Bullhook Road.

Square Butte 3630 [P] From the east. Also known as Box Elder Butte. Four miles northeast of Box Elder.

Centennial Mountain 5806 [D] Communications site.

Bowery Peak 6150 [P] Lookout site.

■ **Baldy Mountain 6916** [W] Take Highway 234 south out of Havre for 25 miles. Park at the Teepee Campground, and cross it to find the trail. Climb 2100' in 1½ miles to the top. Another approach can be made by parking on the county road, strolling up grassy slopes on the northeast side of the mountain, and ascending the rocky northeast ridge.

Big John Butte 5956 [S] Southwest ridge.

Murphy Butte 5478 [S] From the northeast.

Corrigan Mountain 5405 [S] From the east.

Sawtooth Mountain 5246 [S] Southeast approach.

Barber Butte 5035 [S] Northeast approach from truck road.

Lloyd Butte 4999 [S]

Timber Butte 5446 [S] Radio facility. West ridge from a truck road.

Black Butte 5566 [S] From the northwest or southeast. Covered with patchy timber. Rocky summit.

Johnson Butte 5207 [S] From the north or east.

Rieve Butte 5392 [S] From truck road to the west along Hanson Creek. Also known as Ram Point.

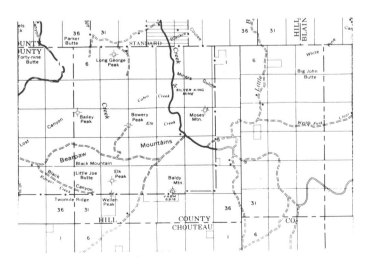

Manshead Rock, a volcanic formation, from the north side of Lloyd Butte

Looking southeast off Lloyd Butte

Suction Butte 5329 [S] North side.

Butte 5435 [S] From the west.

Myrtle Butte 5268 [S] From the north or east.

Miles Butte 4949 [S] West side from truck road.

McCann Butte 4308 [S] South or west side. Road around the base.

Wild Horse Butte 3241 [P] Solitary hill 18 miles north of Hays.

Three Buttes 3855 [W] North of Hays, just west of Highway 66. Trail from the west up the middle one, the highest. Western butte 3854'. Eastern one 3379'.

Thornhill Butte 4636 [S] Scramble from the east to the timbered top. This butte is four miles northwest of the D-Y Highway Junction. While in this area, consider going to the Jim Kipp Overlook for a view of the wild, primitive Missouri River Breaks. On Highway 66 1½ miles north of the D-Y Junction, turn west onto a county road. Follow it about 15 miles. The overlook was dedicated in 1956 by the family and friends of Jim Kipp, and from it you can see the Cow Creek area where Chief Joseph crossed the river on the way to his last battle in the Bearpaws. Jim was the son of Indian and white parents. He began ranching his homestead in 1913 with his young bride Octavia. Until his death in March 1956 he earned a rigorous living, and extended friendship and assistance to every man, white or Indian. In his later years he liked to take strangers to the point now named for him to hear the exclamations of those who had never before seen the country. Jim would have made a good mountain guide, and his overlook embodies the strangeness and beauty that prevails over the Montana prairie.

THE LITTLE ROCKY MOUNTAINS

The Little Rockies were the scene of mining activity. You can easily slide into open mine shafts just by standing near the edge. Also, the old roads are covered with coarse rocks, each specifically engineered to gouge a tire or mangle a muffler.

Antoine Butte 5725 [P] Radio facilities. A car *can* make it (wrecker service in Hays). Three high points are about the same height, surrounded by impenetrable lodgepole pine scrub.

Shell Butte 5692 [S] From the west.

Old Scraggy Peak 5708 [S] Bushwhack from the northeast.

Ricker Butte 3977 [S] West side from Highway 191. Elevation gain 550'.

Coburn Butte 3784 [S] North shoulder from Highway 191. Ricker Butte to the southwest.

North side of the Eastern Bearpaws. Black Butte, left. Smaller buttes lie in the southern portion of this area.

Northwest side of Suction Butte

Northwest side of Old Scraggy Peak
—U.S. Forest Service

THE LARB HILLS

A broad highland without prominent summits, most abrupt at Hinsdale (2180') where four miles to the south the ground has risen to 2902'.

Ball Rock Point 3140 [J] On Iron Stake Ridge, southeast of Sun Prairie Flats in Section 20, Township 22 North, Range 33 East. Provides a fine view of a remote stretch of Fort Peck Reservoir, 2246', just below.

Tiger Butte 2371 [S] Drive within a mile of this little peak, six miles southeast of Glasgow.

THE HIGHLINE

A broad windswept area north of Highway 2 between Havre and the North Dakota state line. No significant vertical landforms. High points are grassy flats on low-slung bluffs between coulees, and include the Havre Air Force Station (3200'), Cherrypatch Ridge (3590') north of Harlem in Section 26, Township 36 North, Range 21 East, and the old radar base at Opheim (3292'). In winter there is a little more snow, and in spring the drifts are slower to melt than those along the Milk River around 2000'.

Kaminski Hill 3140 [S] Walk up from the north or south. Ten miles northeast of Opheim.

Four Buttes 2635 [S] West of the town of Four Buttes, one mile north of Highway 248. The second one from the south is highest, rising 150' above the surrounding land, a lot in an area where the highest points are grain elevators.

Square Butte 2900 [S] From the north or south. North of Scobey.

Long Butte 2895 [S] From the south. North of Whitetail.

Technical Opportunities: Young granite in the Sweetgrass Hills offers the best chance for a rock climb, though little is exposed. The high prairie setting and the untested (as of this writing) faces indicate a stimulating experience in store. The Bearpaws and Little Rockies have exposed rock, but it is modioore.

Southeast face of West Butte, where the igneous core of this laccolith is exposed. These are the only cliffs in the area.

Mt. Baldy from its north ridge

The Dry Range, surrounded by ranchland   *Willow Mountain from the northwest*

The Big Belt Mountains

"No person who has yet to discover some of the pleasures of climbing can possibly realize the intangibles associated with a day on the mountain."

—J. Gordon Edwards

Description: A long, broad dissected range with a 5700' elevation span. Ridgetops sparsely timbered.

Geology: Limestone and Precambrian sediments over exposed basement rocks make up this uplifted dome. The Adel Mountains to the north have weird volcanic formations.

Access: East of Helena. Back roads from Highway 284 are the usual routes. Ridgetops are accessible by truck roads and foot trails.

Ownership: Helena National Forest, ranch companies, small private holdings.

THE ADEL AREA

The Sawteeth 6845 [S] Grassy hill. Approached from the west, up the North Fork of Stickney Creek.

Sieben Point 7093 [S] South ridge from jeep trail originating at the Sieben Ranch. Also known as Rock Slide Mountain. Flat, grassy summit.

Campbell Point 7097 [S]

Dry Range 6546 [J] A low-slung grassy ridge ten miles long.

THE BIG BELT AREA

Willow Mountain 7190 [S] Southeast ridge.

Shellrock Ridge 7866 [S] Southeast shoulder. Grassy top three miles north of Moors Mountain.

Moors Mountain 7980 [S] A timbered dome.

The Missouri River enters the Gates of the Mountains. Hogback Mountain, right skyline   *Mt. Baldy from its north summit*

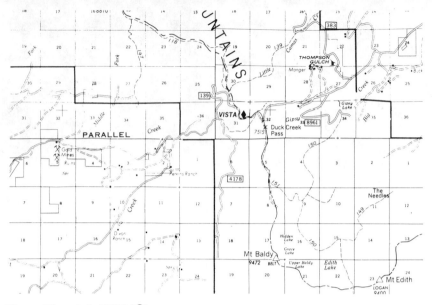

Sheep Mountain 7368 [S]

Hogback Mountain 7813 [D] Maintained lookout.

Avalanche Butte 7701 [S]

Boulder Baldy 8942 [J] Depending on the condition of the trail, you'll probably be better off hiking part of it.

■ **Mt. Baldy 9472** [S] Two miles east of Townsend on Highway 12, turn north onto Highway 284 and drive 11 miles. Then turn east onto Duck Creek Road and follow it 15 miles to Duck Creek Pass. A jeep trail heads south 2½ miles up the north ridge of Mt. Baldy. You'll need a four-wheel drive truck with good ground clearance. Park near the end and start hiking, angling right (west) to get on the west side of the ridge, traversing under or climbing over a grassy point on the ridge. Continue south, drop into a saddle, dodge thickets of trees, and ascend the final ridge over a false peak. The long grassy summit drops abruptly on the east side. Watch for mountain goats. In the summit cairn is a little register in a pill bottle with a childproof cap.

Mt. Edith 9480 [S] Easy stroll from trail to the west.

THE SIXTEENMILE AREA

Grassy Mountain 7687 [W] A stroll through high meadows. Start from Klondike Pass to the south.

Black Butte 6436 [S] South side. This timbered summit is six miles northwest of Ringling, on private land.

Sixmile Mountain 7637 [W] Ten miles east of Toston.

Mt. Edith from the northwest

Grassy Mountain from the northwest

Technical Opportunities: Limestone cliffs, spires, and chimneys adorn the area between Beaver Creek and Avalanche Butte. These formations are rotten even for limestone and their use should be limited to rappelling, unless you like the thrill of clutching your route as your weight peels it off the mountain.

Limestone Cliffs along
Trout Creek
—U.S. Forest Service

Rolls of hay dot long slopes, north side of the Little Belts.

Highwood Baldy. Left: View from the northwest.
Right: Its grassy north ridge from the head of Deer
Creek

The Little Belt Mountains

"But we are not cold; our success makes us feel warm. All our being glows with a noble fire and we rejoice at having been permitted to leave the drudgery of everyday life far below."

—Rudolf Dienst

Description: Low ridge systems sprawl from Kings Hill Pass. High points are mostly on broad timbered ridges, though talus domes east of Neihart are above timberline and span 5700'. In the Highwood group to the north, high slopes are grassy.

Geology: An uplifted sedimentary dome with lots of limestone. The Highwoods are remnants of volcanoes. Igneous intrusions, of which Square Butte is the most striking, occur in both areas.

Access: Southeast of Great Falls. Highway 89 gets close to the more popular peaks. Jeep and foot trails are common. The Highwoods are best approached on the Highwood Creek Road from Highway 228 a mile south of Highwood.

Ownership: Lewis and Clark National Forest.

THE HIGHWOOD MOUNTAINS

Gossack Mountain 5202 [S] Southwest side from Gap Creek Road.
Carter Mountain 5492 [J] From Shonkin Creek.
Windy Mountain 5998 [W] Grassy top. From trail on the south ridge it's ⅛ mile.
Belt Butte 4650 [W] From the east.
Comers Butte 5440 [S] Southwest or east side.
Pinewood Peak 6870 [S] From saddle to the east, gained by trail up the North Fork of Belt Creek. Timbered summit.

East from Highwood Baldy. Highwood Creek, foreground. Prospect Peak extreme left. East Peak right. Arrow Peak far right. Square Butte in the distance, left

Northwest side of South Peak

Square Butte, as it appears from Highway 200 and in many Charlie Russell paintings

Western slopes, Little Belt Mountains

Highwood Baldy 7670 [W] Up Belt Creek on the southwest side from the locked gate. On older maps the trail up the north side is now a cow trail which fades at the head of Deer Creek. It leaves Highwood Creek at a small campsite just before the third drive-thru of the creek, and fades out on the north ridge. At 7000' you'll hit timberline. (The timber is above, not below you.) You may find traces of the old trail in the timber. The top is open, but for all the great views, change positions around the block communications shelter square on the summit.

Middle Peak 7074 [S]

South Peak 7075 [S] Southwest side. Radio towers at 6750'.

Prospect Peak 6549 [S] Southwest ridge from Cottonwood Creek. Grassy top.

Arrow Peak 7485 [S] Bushwhack through timber from a pack trail to the north ridge. Timbered summit. Follow a grassy ridgetop south two miles to Lava Peak, 7142'.

East Peak 7010 [S] Southeast ridge from Fall Creek. Timbered summit.

Round Butte 5370 [S] From the northwest. There are also breaks in the cliffs on the south side.

Square Butte 5703 [S] North side of the east end from a jeep trail. The flat, irregularly shaped top, over 100 acres, rises 1700' over the surrounding plain. Lower slopes are sage brush mosaics interspersed with rattlesnakes. The mountain itself is black, basalt-like volcanic rock under vivid white rock. Geologically it's a laccolith. Once this igneous intrusion cooled under the surface, the overburden eroded away. Volcanic dikes, once exposed, became the outlying pinnacles and spires. Because the mountain stands alone, it looks like the broad side of a barn to passing thunderstorms. The timber never gets very big due to periodic lightning fires. The last big one was in 1956.

Porphyry Peak Lookout

Big Baldy's southwest side and commercial forestland

September on Big Baldy's lofty dome, where hard winds make a snow ghost of an old pole. There once was a primitive telephone lookout on this mountain.

Looking east off Sand Point —Bill Cunningham

THE LITTLE BELTS—WEST OF HIGHWAY 89

Tiger Butte 7001 [S] Southwest ridge.

Strawberry Ridge 7222 [W]

Monument Ridge 7330 [W] From road to the southeast.

Monument Peak 7395 [P] Old lookout site.

Thunder Mountain 8123 [S] From the southeast. Flat timbered summit.

Green Mountain 7544 [W] Truck road ¼ mile down the south side.

Iron Mountain 7762 [S] From roads on the southwest or east side.

Woods Mountain 7525 [S] South ridge. A timbered plateau.

Rimrock Ridge 7195 [J] A ridge of open grass three miles long, reached from the Tenderfoot Creek-Park Creek Divide, or via the road up Strawberry Gulch which ends above Deadman Gulch at 6875'.

Williams Mountain 7595 [P] Old lookout site.

■ **Porphyry Peak 8192** [D] Just north of Kings Hill Pass on Highway 89, turn west on Road #838 and follow it 1½ miles. In the winter, a chairlift also goes to the summit. This is a great place to take the family for panoramic views of central Montana. From the manned lookout you can sometimes pick out the Sweetgrass Hills near the Canadian border, and Mt. Cowan just north of the Wyoming state line.

Park Hills 6610 [P] A highland five miles north of White Sulphur Springs.

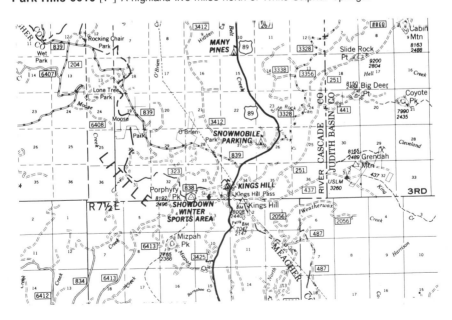

Limestone Butte 5865 [P] Approach from the northeast.

Barker Mountain 8309 [S] East ridge from end of jeep trail out of the old mining town of Barker.

Mixes Baldy 7952 [S] North saddle from Daisy Creek to the west.

Anderson Peak 7687 [W] Old lookout site. Walk old road (not on new map) starting in the north of Section 16.

Granite Mountain 7636 [S] South ridge.

Butcherknife Mountain 7944 [W] North ridge trail from saddle at the head of Blankenship Gulch.

Neihart Baldy 8286 [S] West side from a gated jeep trail starting across the highway from the Neihart School.

Long Mountain 8621 [S] From Neihart Baldy or prospects on the north side.

Big Baldy Mountain 9175 [S] Register. Basically a walk, but the trail on the summit dome crosses jagged rock fields and is marked only by cairns. Park where Road #3328 crosses Chamberlain Creek for the shortest approach up the southwest shoulder.

Bandbox Mountain 8100 [W] South ridge from trail.

Yogo Peak 8801 [J] Old lookout site.

Kelly Mountain 8153 [W]

Grendah Mountain 8165 [S] Short scramble from a truck road ½ mile southwest.

Sand Point 8211 [P] A scenic ridgetop knob.

Ettien Ridge 7570 [P]

Mt. High 8242 [P] Old lookout site.

Daisy Peak 7782 [W]

Volcano Butte 6225 [S] South side.

Technical Opportunities: Marginal formations along the Missouri River include Citadel, Hole-in-the-Wall, Chimney Rock, and Black Rock. Limited excellent granite is found in the Carpenter Creek Intrusion just north of Neihart. A step down in quality, but perhaps more aesthetic are the volcanics and unusual intrusives around Square Butte. Almost everywhere else, one is confounded by striking cliffs of rancid limestone.

Crisp granite east of Highway 89 between Monarch and Neihart

Prairie and mountains meet, north side of the Judiths.

The Snowy Mountains

"I can see far down the mountain
*   Where I've wandered many years,*
Often hindered on my journey
*   By the ghosts of doubts and fears;*
Broken vows and disappointments
*   Thickly strewn along the way,*
But the spirit led unerring
*   To the land I hold today."*

—A. N. Trotter

Description: The Big Snowy formation is a broad east-west ridge, heavily buttressed by side ridges, with no dominant feature on its grassy top. Elevation drops southward 5300'. The Judith and Moccasin mountains are tidy little ranges of timber interspersed with grassy openings.

Geology: The Snowies are a dome uplift of sedimentary formations. The Judiths and Moccasins are of volcanic origin. Laccoliths of an oddball igneous rock form each major peak of the Judiths.

Access: Around Lewistown. County and ranch roads go to the outlying hills. Best route into the Judiths is through Maiden from Highway 191. Easiest trail into the Big

South Moccasins from Judith Peak

Judith Peak, accessible to all vehicles and a good place to take the family. However, don't leave children unattended around the old buildings.

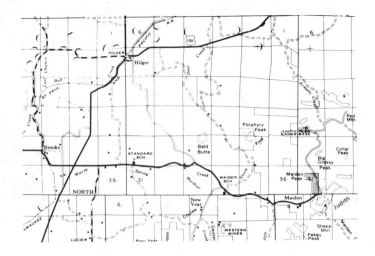

Snowies begins at Crystal Lake. A county road to the lake (watch for sign) leaves Highway 200 nine miles west of Lewistown.

Ownership: Lewis and Clark National Forest (Snowies), Lewistown District Bureau of Land Management (Judith-Moccasins).

THE MISSOURI BREAKS AREA

Baker Monument 3198 [W] From jeep trail to the east. A small prominent hill 20 miles east of Winifred.

THE MOCCASIN MOUNTAINS

North Moccasin Point 5581 [S] From end of jeep road to the southwest.
South Point 5798 [P] From south or east. Radio facilities.

THE JUDITH MOUNTAINS

■ **Judith Peak 6428** [D] Turn east off Highway 191 ten miles north of Lewistown onto the paved road to Maiden. Past Maiden the road becomes double-lane gravel, climbing a mile to a junction in a saddle. Bear left on the double lane, going three more miles to the top, where you'll find ruins of an abandoned radar base, a valuable archaeological site representative of primitive military civilization in the 1960s. The headquarters is a building within a building, being enclosed in two walls of thick concrete. The structure was apparently designed to withstand a nearby nuclear explosion, as if there'd be anything worth coming out for afterwards. This mountaintop is a good place to contemplate storms wielding their power as they sweep across Pleistocene skies, as well as world governments and where they derive their power.

Black Butte 5585 [S] Park to the west and cross prairie to the curved draw ascending northeast on the west face. Head up this draw. There's an intermittent trail through the trees.
Pyramid Peak 6127 [S] Northwest ridge from truck road.

West side of Black Butte

Typical scenery in the Big Snowies —Bill Cunningham

On the Big Snowy Crest
—Bill Cunningham

THE BIG SNOWY MOUNTAINS

West Peak 8211 [W] Radio facilities. This "peak" is the west end of the Big Snowy Crest.
Greathouse Peak 8681 [W] The trail starts from Crystal Lake, climbs to the Big Snowy Crest, and heads east through mangled thickets of trees interspersed between large expanses of alpine prairie. The crest narrows to a few feet at Knife Blade Ridge. There are other surprises.
Big Snowy Mountain 8678 [W] Trail #649 is a jeep trail sometimes driveable partways. The new Forest Service map calls this peak "Old Baldy." Nonsense. There are dozens of Baldys in the state already. There must be something else to call a mountain without trees on top. Climbers revolt! Unite against any more Baldy Mountains. This is Big Snowy Mountain—a nice name, an appropriate name, and a name with historical basis. Defend it.

THE LITTLE SNOWY MOUNTAINS

Little Snowy Mountain 6250 [P] The Little Snowies are a broad rise of grass and scattered trees, with a truck road to the highest portions.

THE MUSSELSHELL RIVER AREA

The Cayuse Hills range from 4000' to 5615'. There are no prominent summits in this intriguing, complex layout of low-profiles.

Pole Point 3802 [S] High point of the Naderman Buttes 12 miles west of Roundup. Road ½ mile west or one mile east.

Technical Opportunities: The only halfway-solid rock is found in resistant igneous formations on the south sides of Judith Peak and Black Butte.

Igneous outcrops, south side Judith Peak

Southern peaks, Bridger Range, from the north

Sacajawea Peak, showing the final stretch of trail. Multiple points of Hardscrabble Peak beyond to the north

Imposing lousy limestone graces the east side of Sacajawea Peak.

The Bridger Range

"In the heart of every mountaineer there is . . . room both for a very difficult first ascent and for the contemplation of a flower."

—Gaston Rebuffat

Description: Small, isolated, abrupt, and steep. Upper slopes of loose rock well above timberline. Farm and ranchland valleys 5600' below.

Geology: An uplift of limestone (rich in fossils) and other Precambrian sediments.

Access: North of Bozeman. Dirt roads and trails branch off Highway 86. Some approaches cross private land.

Ownership: Gallatin National Forest.

Garden Point 7133 [W] Jeep road ¼ mile away. Southwest of Maudlow. High point in the Horseshoe Hills.

Blacktail Mountain 8383 [S] South ridge west of Gallop Creek. Possible by horse.

Hatfield Mountain 7615 [J]

Hardscrabble Peak 9501 [S] Register. South ridge from trail in saddle west of Fairy Lake. Third peak north on ridge is highest.

■ **Sacajawea Peak 9670** [W] Register. Take Highway 86 north out of Bozeman. Past Bridger Bowl Ski Area the road turns into gravel. After six miles turn left onto Forest Road #74 for the final five miles to Fairy Lake. Hike the trail two miles to the saddle north of the peak, then on to the top. Or climb the east ridge to the summit ridge about a mile south of the peak.

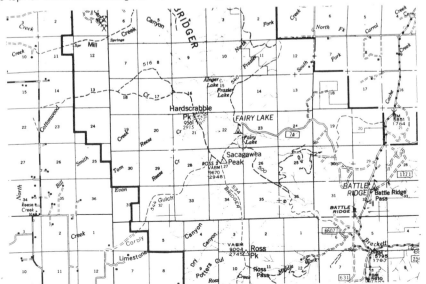

Upturned slabs. North face of Ross Peak, upper left

Ross Peak 9004 [C] Register. The easiest way is to gain Ross Pass from Brackett Creek to the east, then hike north, passing the peak on its west side. Head up the northwest ridge. You can also slog up the steep east side. The north side is technical. Western approaches cross private land.

Saddle Peak 9162 [S] Register. Head up Maynard Creek, in the Bridger Bowl Ski Area. Approaches up Slushman or Truman creeks cross private land.

Baldy Mountain 8900 [S] Register. Try the north ridge, or the southwest ridge from the "M."

Angell Point 7964 [J] Short walk from road to the east. This road outslopes menacingly, and four-wheel drive is advisable, though a two-wheel drive truck can get close under dry conditions. Angell Point dominates the Bangtail area of broad grassy ridgetops.

Technical Opportunities: Limestone is the only exposed rock, and is usually on the east side of peaks and ridges. Without pushing the difficulty of a route, one can find interesting and scenic action. This is not the place for the more exposed lines or the use of direct aid.

looking south into the central Crazies

The Crazy Mountains

"Senile fellows, backed by brass,
Ridges, fissures, crags entire
Defined in contrast, audible–
Sceneries merge to memories while they are still before us: Prefaced,
*   As lack to seems, or fact to dreams."*
— From a poem by the author, 1970

Description: Isolated, jagged, unvegetated peaks with sharp, deeply cut canyons and an immediate 7100' elevation span. Long steep slopes of loose talus, broken stretches of cliffs. Broad, vegetated lower summits at the north end. The Castle Mountains are a timbered plateau.

Geology: The south portion was a chain of volcanoes 50 million years ago and is now a chaos of glaciated volcanics. To the north are unglaciated 100-million-year-old sediments with 50-million-year-old igneous intrusions. The Castles are an unglaciated granite plug surrounded by younger sediments.

Access: North of Livingston. Ranch roads approach from Highway 89 (west side) and Highway 191 (east side). Trails head up the largest drainages into the peaks. Back roads get closer to the summits in the northern end, and in the Castles.

Ownership: Gallatin and Lewis and Clark national forests, checkerboarded with private holdings.

Background: The Crazies are the most primitive, forbidding mountains in the state. The ridges, bare bones of God's green earth, are obviously on poor terms with most forms of plant life. The absence of an even half-hearted mountain serenity on such a

Loco Peak. Castle Mountains on horizon to the northwest

Lebo Peak. Shields Valley to the west

Sunlight Lake. Sunlight Peak behind

Conical Peak from the southeast. Trail to Conical Pass (left) easily visible

grand scale is awesome, as the range makes not even a pretense of hospitality. Ascents are nothing harder than scrambles, but these are hard scrambles. The peaks are remote, the routes long, and the footing is, though variable, never firm. What one finds in this desolation is best evidenced by vision quest sites found on a few summits. These consist of rock rings (now protected by law) placed by Indians not very long ago. It would be interesting to come across one of these sites, but once in these mountains you may want to go up and establish your own.

THE CASTLE MOUNTAINS

Elk Peak 8566 [J] Southeast of White Sulphur Springs. A flat timbered dome.

THE SHIELDS RIVER AREA

Unknown Point 8311 [W] Grassy top.

Scab Rock Mountain 7894 [S] Central peak of Tri-Peaks Mountain, best climbed on the west side. Bear Mountain, 7805', lies a mile north and can be climbed from the saddle between the two peaks. Goat Mountain, 7770', can be done on its southeast side.

Virginia Peak 8775 [S] Climb the west ridge for ¼ mile from the Eagle Creek trail.

Loco Peak 9239 [W] Uplift of prairie 9000' high and two miles long. Good ways are the east or southeast ridges from Lebo Fork of Big Elk Creek. A longer, prettier trip is the trail from the west or northeast.

Lebo Peak 9004 [S] North ridge from Lebo Fork of Big Elk Creek.

Porcupine Butte 7010 [J] From the west. On private land.

THE CRAZY MOUNTAINS—MAIN GROUP

Sunlight Peak 10090 [S] The south side from Middle Fork of Sweetgrass Creek is safest. The north ridge, more convenient, can be gained either from Sunlight Lake or Sunlight Creek. Near the summit the ridgetop is rated C.

North side of Granite Peak. Iddings Peak, upper left

East face of Peak 10578. In the foreground is Peak 10452, on the ridge connecting Peak 10437 with Iddings Peak.

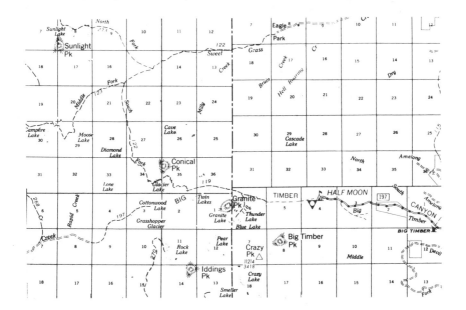

■ **Conical Peak 10748** [S] Drive 11 miles north of Big Timber on Highway 191, then turn west onto Big Timber Creek Road and drive to Half Moon campground at the end. You'll now climb 4000' in 6½ miles. Trail #119 starts as an old mining road, hard work for two miles. Then it narrows, becomes even more difficult, but is easy to follow. After 4½ miles, once around the sheer north side of Granite Mountain to timberline, you'll find Twin Lakes, a lush foreground under talus slopes and jagged peaks. Onward from the lake, it's 1½ miles to Conical Pass (10200'), through an elaborate array of switchbacks, rock meadows, snowdrifts, and ledges. A final half-hour scramble up the south ridge climbs around or over small outcrops to the summit. It's a great view from this centrally located point, especially of the broad pyramid of Crazy Peak with its dramatic buttresses of aretes and scree.

Peak 10482 [S] West of Glacier Lake. Head up the cirque on the south side, starting just below Cottonwood Lake.

Peak 10437 [S] South side from Rock Lake. Located southwest of Twin Lakes, it guards Grasshopper Glacier cirque.

Peak 10578 [S] West of Rock Lake. Scramble up the southwest face after crossing over from Rock Creek through a saddle on the southwest spur.

Granite Peak 10132 [S] Register. The normal route is the southeast side. The north slopes and east ridge have technical routes with alternative C-rated routes. A few years back a climber with a broken leg was rescued from the east ridge.

Iddings Peak 10936 [C] West ridge from Rock Lake easiest. Southeast ridge from Smeller Lake has more rock climbing.

Crazy Peak 11214 [S] Register. To try the east ridge, get permission to drive up the Middle Fork of Big Timber Creek. Try the house in Section 16 just south of Big Timber Creek, then drive up Devil Creek to the highest point of this primitive road. Head west up through the timber. A compass and topographic map will help. Within a mile, drop to the south (left) and cross the Middle Fork.

Iddings Peak from the east   *Iddings Peak from the south*   **181**

Crazy Peak's long east ridge

Northeast side of Crazy Peak's summit, showing "The Surprise" on the west ridge route, and the top of the permanent snow couloir

Now hike the ascending timbered ridge on the south side of the creek a mile to where the east buttress opens up. Climb it to the east ridge and grind on to the summit. It'll take a while. Another popular route is the west ridge, reached by climbing south from Blue Lake to a saddle, then following the west ridge to what looks like the summit, but—surprise—is a false summit separated from the top by a steep gash. Descend the south side of the false summit to get in a gully, rated C, that goes up the true summit. On the northeast side of the gash is a steep gully of technical ice and snow. The traverse on the northeast ridge from Big Timber Peak is strictly for roped teams.

Big Timber Peak 10795 [S] Northeast ridge from Big Timber Creek.

Peak 10840 (Jeanie Peak) [S] Located at the head of the South Forks of Big Timber Creek. Try the north side from Crazy or Smeller lakes, or the east ridge.

Peak 10560 (Swamp Lake Peak) [S] East ridge, or the south ridge from the spur on the southwest side of Swamp Lake (nestled on the southeast side of the peak).

Fairview Peak 10164 [S] North side from Swamp Lake.

Swamp Lake and Swamp Lake Peak

South end of the Crazies. Fairview Peak, left foreground

Technical Opportunities: There are some short walls in the valleys. More common are long, rugged aretes of moderate exposure on the sides of the peaks and ridges. Snow couloirs and glacier remnants are readily found in the higher areas. There's an unusual metamorphic plug above Rock Lake, just west of Grasshopper Glacier. Rock quality improves in the west half of the Castles, where small granite spires are scattered. Some are on the west fringe of the uplift, where access is across private land.

South face of Iddings Peak, with both steep rock arêtes and ice couloirs

South from the summit of Gallatin Peak. The metal box mounted on a rock is a Forest Service register.

North Fork of Hell Roaring Creek. North side of
Gallatin Peak, left —U.S. Forest Service

South side of Point 10640, middle distance. Gallatin
Peak, right

The Madison Range

"Stood on a ridge and shunned religion, thinking the world was mine.
Made my break and a big mistake, stealin' when I should have been buyin'."
—Ken Hensley

Description: A spectacular medley of graceful scree summits and startling pinnacles. Timberline at 9000', gentle slopes of grass and moss extending higher. Elevation span 6500'.

Geology: This fault block of basement rock saw scattered volcanic activity. Eroded material was deposited in large alluvial fans on the west side. Intrusions produced granitics in the south half of the Spanish Peaks. An igneous band also runs through the Taylor-Hilgard area.

Access: Southwest of Bozeman. Dirt and gravel roads poke in from Highway 87 (west side) and Highway 191 (east side). Highway 64 is paved to the base of Lone Mountain. Elsewhere, trails serve the higher regions.

Ownership: Beaverhead and Gallatin national forests.

THE SPANISH PEAKS AREA

Red Mountain 5726 [S] East ridge from the Madison River. Northeast of Norris.

Salesville Point 7245 [S] Via Browns Gulch from the Gallatin River to the east.

Point 10742, "The Beehive," from the
south. Blaze Mountain just beyond

The west side of Gallatin Peak,
showing route from Thompson Lake

Wilson Peak from the northwest

East side of Fan Mountain

Anceney Point 9800 [W] Old jeep trail to 9370' on the northwest ridge.

Point 10175 [S] East face from Jerome Rock Lakes.

Blaze Mountain 10400 [S] Interesting routes include the northeast ridge from Mirror Lake, the north ridge, and the northwest slopes. A long streak of snow called "The Blaze" remains on the west side all summer.

Point 10742 (The Beehive) [C] Register. This granite crag usually approached from Beehive Basin. Climb a steep gully to a notch, west of the peak, separating it from the south ridge. Early in summer the gully is full of snow. From the notch head up a steeper gully to the ridgetop. Traverse right to the summit. Another route of similar difficulty, but more exposed, is the east ridge, done from a saddle reached from Beehive Lake. You might want a rope for belaying. The north and south faces are definitely technical, with variable difficulty on the many lines of ascent.

Point 10660 [S] South ridge from Chilled Lakes.

Point 10640 [S] Southwest ridge from Chilled Lakes.

Beacon Point 10248 [W] A trail tops the ridge east of the peak.

Gallatin Peak 11015 [S] Register. The west side is the simplest of several scrambling routes. Find a grassy gully ¼ mile southwest of Thompson Lake and follow it through a cirque carpeted with spongy moss to a broad gully ending on top.

Jumbo Mountain 10416 [S] South ridge from Hell Roaring Lake, the southeast side, or the broad north shoulder.

Wilson Peak 10700 [C] Register. Usual approach up the east ridge, gained from trail above Hell Roaring Lake. You may prefer to belay on the pointed summit. The north face has technical options.

Table Mountain 9840 [W]

THE WEST FORK AREA

Fan Mountain 10304 [S] Register. The northwest ridge of the west peak is easiest. Once on the west peak (9844') head east one mile on the connecting ridge. Other interesting routes are the northwest ridge of the main peak, the southeast ridge, or a spur on the south side.

Lone Mountain 11166 [S] Register. The east or southwest ridges are best. A snow gully on the northeast side is technical. The Big Sky Ski Area runs its gondola sometimes in summer to the

A spectacular lookout once stood on Lone Mountain.
Photo taken July 1921 —U.S. Forest Service

Lone Mountain from the northeast

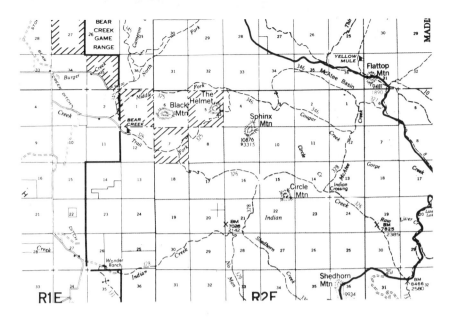

base of the east ridge, 9000'. In winter a chairlift operates in good weather to 9800'. Angle left from there, climbing to where the east ridge steepens under the peak. Notify the ski area before attempting this route. The east ridge is often shot with a howitzer for avalanche control and is closed to keep adventurers like you out of the line of fire and off unstable snows.

Cedar Mountain 10800 [S] Register (southwest peak). Any approach will gain the main horseshoe-shaped ridge. The southwest peak is highest, the southeast peak is 10779'. Good routes are the north ridge, the west ridge, the southwest corner, or from Cedar Lake.

Pioneer Mountain 9861 [S] Register. From the west.

The Helmet 9647 [S] Southwest side.

■ **Sphinx Mountain 10876** [S] Turn east off Highway 287 at Cameron and go 9½ miles, following signs, to the Bear Creek Ranger Station. Park, and tear up Trail #326. In two miles take a left at a junction, and follow Trail #325 up to the saddle between Sphinx Mountain and The Helmet. Charge up the great grassy gully splitting the northwest corner of this mountain to the summit plateau. On top is a register. Henry Hall reported finding a register in 1918 with an undated entry by a Japanese party. Evidently a rancher in the Madison Valley had Japanese guests prior to then, and they made one of the first recorded climbs of a major peak in Montana.

Cinnamon Mountain 9238 [W] Old lookout building.

THE TAYLOR-HILGARD AREA

No Man Peak 10843 [S] Register. Northwest ridge.

The Wedge 10699 [C]

Koch Peak 11286 [S] Register. The southeast ridge is the normal route. The west ridge is also a scramble. The north ridge looks like a scramble, but lurking near the summit is the "Notch in Koch," called other things. This gap is rated hard C, with a belay advisable.

Northeast side of Cedar Mountain   *Northwest corner of Sphinx Mountain*   187

South side of Koch Peak

West side of Koch Peak and the north ridge, showing the gap where unsuspecting scramblers have either turned back or quickly increased climbing skills

Finger Mountain 10808 [S] South side west of Finger Lakes.

Imp Peak 11212 [S] Register. East peak is highest. The east face has a couple of technical pitches.

Woodward Mountain 10670 [S] Most climbs up the east side. Other approaches, all scrambles, vary greatly in terrain. Consider going up and down opposite sides to check out limestone formations on the west side.

Echo Peak 11214 [S] Register. Scramble up the southwest side or the north ridge. The north ridge steepens near the top. A more complicated route, depending on snow conditions, threads its way up the northeast side.

Dutchman Peak 10991 [S] South ridge gained at a saddle from the east. Technical climbing from the north.

Hilgard Peak 11316 [C] Both Hilgard and North Hilgard (a few feet shorter) have registers. Hilgard wasn't climbed until 1949. North Hilgard, a technical climb from any side, waited until 1956. Since then they've remained remote.

Hilgard is one of those difficult-looking mountains where the route opens up once you get started. However, there is only one way, straight and narrow, that can be done without technical equipment. Get on the southeast side of the peak. If approaching from the northeast, climb a couloir on the east ridge (not the couloir next to the peak) to get over on the south side of this ridge, then head for the top of the talus slope on the southeast face of Hilgard. Locate a way straight up the face, which has three crags at the top. None of these crags is the summit, which is located behind the right one. Reach the gap between the central and right-hand crag. Then head over the right crag, traverse a moderately exposed slab, and there you are. Another possible route is the south ridge, about as easy except for one 12' drop. Warning: If these routes become wet while you are on top, you cannot descend without rappelling gear. If rain approaches, leave immediately. The steep, slick rock and threat of lightning are extremely dangerous.

There are several technical routes. Bolts have been used, but nuts work well. Use them instead—this is a wilderness peak. The west side has challenging lines, but the northeast direct route is probably the favorite. Use a rope as you head up the east gully for the notch between Hilgard and North Hilgard. Since the rope pulls rocks off, you'll need rock helmets, too. Once at the notch, stash rope and helmets, unless you plan to rappel off the northeast or northwest side of the summit.

East side of Woodward Mountain Koch Peak, right horizon

What it's all about—the summit world. On White Peak, a point on Redstreak Peak's southeast ridge —Bill Cunningham

Imp Peak, southeast side

Imp Peak, northwest side.

Echo Peak, southwest side

Echo Peak, northeast side

North Hilgard is easiest climbed from the notch by way of a traverse from Hilgard, though climbing up the gully to reach the notch certainly works. From the notch to the top, consider a rope for belaying. The moves aren't that hard, but exposure the last 60' is unrelenting. The north side is a definite challenge for the serious craigsman.

Monument Peak 10091 [W]

Sage Peak 10664 [S] Come up the west slope, as the east side has an abrupt cliff. Stay on the ridgetop where the trail from the west drops off southward. Climb eastward over a false peak, 9700', descend the other side 300', then head on up the final west slope.

Redstreak Peak 10384 [S] Register. Southwest side.

Northeast side, chiseled igneous towers of Hilgard Peak

Lionhead Peaks from the northeast.
Point 10609, center, and east side of
Sheep Mountain, right

Sheep Mountain from the northwest —U.S. Forest
Service

THE LIONHEAD AREA

Sheep Mountain 10311 [S] East side easiest.

Point 10609 [S] A large, flat-topped mountain on the south ridge of Sheep Mountain.

Black Mountain 10237 [S] Shown on some maps as Reynolds Point. Northeast ridge from head of Mile Creek. W-rated if done from the Idaho side.

Bald Peak 10180 [S] Lionhead Point on some maps. Northeast ridge from a saddle below the peak.

Lionhead Mountain 9574 [S] Trail from the east,

Technical Opportunities: Besides the steeper routes mentioned on the preceding peaks, there are technical traverses on Tunnel Ridge, Sawtooth Ridge, and The Wedge in the Taylor Peaks area. The northern end of the Madisons has areas of low-elevation outcrops suitable for practice and project climbing. Along the Madison River east of Norris is "Neatrock," a formation of reddish, twisted granite. It's reached on a mile or so of dirt road heading north from Highway 289 on the west side of the Madison River bridge. The rock has some exfoliation. There are also boulders on the west side of the Gallatin River in the vicinity of the long straight stretch of Highway 191 just north of Gallatin Canyon. Heading up the canyon, a swarm of granite walls and towers flanks the river just south of Squaw Creek. Gallatin Tower, the largest formation on the west side of the highway, has been climbed for many years. Its east face, four pitches, readily accepts nuts. In the back-country, scattered boulders and cliffs of interest can be found in the Spanish Peaks and Hilgard Peak areas.

This buttress glowers over
the North Fork of the West
Fork of the Gallatin River,
just south of the Spanish
Peaks.

Gallatin Tower—Crisp rock
in a crisp morning

Looking south over the Gallatin Range.
Hyalite Ridge, foreground

The Gallatin Range

"The mountains shall bring peace to the people."

—Psalms 72:3

Description: Alpine buttes cluster along the crest of a dissected plateau. Elevation span 6800', though most summit views drop about 5800'.

Geology: This fault block had volcanoes its entire length. Resulting mud and lava flows formed a matrix of rock and petrified wood.

Access: South of Bozeman. Only trails serve the high country. Major trailheads are in Hyalite Canyon (Road #62, reached from Highway 345) and Tom Miner Basin (Road #63, reached from Highway 89, 19 miles north of Gardiner).

Ownership: Gallatin National Forest.

Mt. Ellis 8331 [S] Register. Unmapped trail up the east side, with a grassy stroll from the end to the top. Other routes include the north ridge, and the southwest side from Bozeman Creek.

Wineglass Mountain 8038 [W] Also called Canyon Mountain. Timbered top. The high point is on the west end of the summit ridge.

Storm Castle 7300 [W] Overlooks the Gallatin River above Squaw Creek. Trail starts from the Squaw Creek Road.

Garnet Mountain 8245 [W] Maintained lookout building.

Mt. Blackmore 10154 [W] Register.

Gray Mountain 10035 [S] Best from the west.

Abbott Mountain 10195 [S] Elephant Mountain on some maps. Climb from Palace Lake Basin. Other approaches rated C.

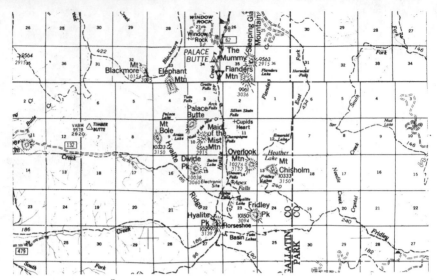

White Mountain 10272 [S] Register. Also known as Liberty Cap. One of the more difficult peaks in the Hyalite area. South ridge from Boles Peak. Depending on route, a little C-rated terrain near the top.

Boles Peak 10333 [S] Register. Mt. Bole on some maps. Gain the south ridge from the Squaw Creek trail.

Arden Peak 10203 [S] From the south.

Maid of the Mist Mountain 9563 [S] Register. Ascend a creek draining around to the east side of the mountain to get behind this peak.

Divide Peak 10038 [W] Southwest ridge. From Squaw Creek trail to the top is ⅓ mile.

Squaw Mountain 10073 [W] Go ⅓ mile up the northeast ridge from a trail.

■ **Hyalite Peak 10299** [W] Drive 21 miles from Bozeman to the end of the Hyalite Creek Road. Head south out of Bozeman just west of Montana State University (Highway 345), turn right after five miles, then turn left into Hyalite Canyon in another mile. The trailhead is a couple of miles past Hyalite Reservoir. Watch for signs. Walk, or ride a horse five miles to Hyalite Lake, 8850'. Find the trail on the west side of this lake which goes 1½ miles to the top. Just before the summit, the trail reaches the saddle between it and Big Chief Mountain, 10202', off to the right (west). Hyalite Peak has a register. The view of the Hyalite area shows volcanic debris landscaped by the wild hand of time and alpine vegetation.

Garnet Mountain Lookout. Gallatin Peak, Spanish Peaks, on skyline

Boles Peak, west side. Fresh snow on August 21.

Boles Peak, east side. Sphinx Mountain, in the Madisons, center horizon

Northeast side of Divide Peak

Palisade Mountain 9422 [S] Register. Southeast ridge, or the northwest side.

The Mummy 9563 [S] North ridge usually used.

Flanders Mountain 9961 [S] North ridge after reaching the Flanders—Mummy saddle from Flanders Lake.

Gail Peak 10161 [S] From Emerald Lake.

Overlook Mountain 10276 [S] Register. From Fridley Lake.

Mt. Chisholm 10333 [S] West ridge, reached from Fridley Lake.

Fridley Peak 10150 [S] Register. South side from Twin Lakes, or the southwest ridge from Hyalite Peak.

Moose Point 10095 [W]

Point 10061 [W] Next to Point 10054, shown on Forest Service maps.

The Sentinel 9946 [W]

Eaglehead Mountain 9976 [W] Radio facilities.

Steamboat Mountain 10023 [S] North ridge.

Twin Peaks 10222 [S] The south peak, 10171', accessible from Ramshorn Peak.

Ramshorn Peak 10289 [W] Register. Millions of years ago an outburst of volcanic activity buried several square miles of timberland under debris. Recent erosion has removed soil generated from volcanic mud and ash, exposing more resistant petrified wood, rock formed from the ancient forest. You need a Forest Service permit to collect petrified wood.

Big Horn Peak 9930 [W]

Sheep Mountain 10095 [W] Scramble from Tom Miner Basin to the north.

North side of Hyalite Peak (left, center). Big Chief Mountain, right of it

Electric Peak, west side

Electric Peak, southeast side

Electric Peak 10992 [S] In Yellowstone National Park. The Park Service recommends a party of four or larger to keep bears away. If coming through the park from the south, the southwest side is a good route. Otherwise the northwest ridge is easiest. The southeast ridge or northeast side also works. If coming up the west, cross over the west peak, 10943', and follow the connecting ridge. In July of 1872 a Geological Survey team ascended the peak and got caught in a thunderstorm. Soon a loud crackling buzz filled the air, and the men felt tingling sensations as current began to pass through their bodies. Finally, one man was severely shocked. The group retreated, then named the peak.

Technical Opportunities: Rock climbing areas in the lower valleys include limestone towers south of Bozeman Pass, but they aren't particularly sound. Volcanic rocks are mostly useless, but there are a few sound outcrops, including Chimney Rock in Pine Creek. Granite along the Gallatin River was mentioned in the Madison Range chapter. A popular granite practice area is on the east side of Hyalite Creek, before the reservoir. Past the reservoir are good winter ice climbs.

40' dihedral on a practice rock in Hyalite Ca

194

A late afternoon in August, the mountains in their prime. Looking south into the Mt. Wallace area

The Absaroka Range—West

"Self-confrontation and inner conflict, though only part of the sport, are nevertheless an inevitable part."

—Royal Robbins

Description: Jagged crags and alpine mesas, sudden and extensive. The north has rugged ridges, rock summits, and long steep slopes, and it immediately rises 7100'. The south, more visually pleasing, has gentler slopes of scattered timber and meadows leading up to assorted odd formations.

Geology: Following heavy volcanic activity, a mighty intrusion produced granite from Mt. Cowan northward.

Access: South of Livingston. Trails serve all high areas and originate from roads along the Yellowstone and Boulder rivers. Mill Creek Road #486 from Highway 540 serves trailheads to the central range, including the Mt. Cowan area.

Ownership: Gallatin National Forest.

Livingston Peak 9314 [S] Northeast side ¼ mile from trail on Baldy Basin Divide.

Elephanthead Mountain 9431 [S] Register. Leave trail to come up the north side. Early in the season there's a snow face here. Leave trail on the east side for a C-rated climb through limestone.

Elephanthead Mountain, left foreground, from the south

Black Mountain, southeast ridge in foreground

Rugged dry mountains north of Cowan

West side of Dexter Point

Shell Mountain 9383 [S] Southwest side from trail, dodging limestone cliffs.

Blacktail Peak 10228 [S] Register. North ridge from Blacktail Lake. Peak not shown on Forest Service map.

Mt. Delano 10138 [S] Register. Northwest ridge or the south side.

Mt. McKnight 10310 [S] Register.

Black Mountain 10941 [S] Register. Scramble southeast from Pine Creek Lake onto the northeast buttress of the southeast ridge. Stay atop the buttress and ridge. Another scrambling route goes up the northwest ridge. The north face is technical, including a long couloir with about five pitches of 60-degree ice in summer.

Marten Peak 10628 [S] Register. All routes are remote affairs. It is possible to climb it as a traverse (rated C) on the northwest ridge from Black Mountain. Bring a rope if you are uncomfortable with a little exposure.

Northeast side of Mt. Cowan, a mountain unlke any other in the state

View from the northeast of spires on Cowan's south ridge. The entire east ridge resembles a foot, with Cowan's summit the big toe. These other four toes are called Eeny, Meeny, Miney, and Mo.

196

Looking southeast off the top of Mt. Cowan

Northwest side of The Pyramid, summit in cloud shadow. Crow Mountain in middle distance

Mt. Rae 9237 [S] Register. Northeast ridge from the divide where a trail comes up from the Main Boulder Ranger Station.

West Boulder Point 10640 [S] Head up from trail to the south.

Dexter Point 10154 [S] Try either the west ridge or the avalanche chute on the southwest side. Note: Access from the west crosses private land.

Mt. Cowan 11206 [C] Register. The summit is on the northeast corner of a giant granitic horseshoe opening to the south. At the northwest corner of the horseshoe is Strawberry Mountain, 11000'—not on the Forest Service map, but it has a register. As for Cowan, its northeast arête is an appealing technical route. The north and east faces are also technical, with the east being quite committing. An ice climb can be made up the north side to the west ridge, where the ascent can be finished non-technically.

Cowan has only one non-technical route, quite complex. It wouldn't be fair to tell all about this unusual wilderness peak, but understand it ain't no debutante. The following points provide critical information, but you can still expect to give your route-finding and rockmanship abilities a workout: 1. The southernmost spire of the south ridge is the impressive peak dominating the north shore of Elbow Lake. The route runs along the base of the south ridge on the left (west) side. 2. You want to end up at a small, usually snow-choked pothole just southwest of the summit pinnacle of Cowan. Climb too high on the south ridge and you will be stranded, like so many before you, at a deep notch separating Cowan from the rest of the south ridge. The pothole shouldn't be confused with the larger lake just over the rocks to the west. 3. You'll be looking for a steep gully on the south side of the west ridge which angles right to about where the west ridge joins the summit pinnacle. If you make this climb before August, take an ice ax for protection on the snow slopes around the pothole. 4. Finally, make a traverse across the southwest face of the pinnacle, and then an ascending traverse coming back to the west edge of the pinnacle. Locate a ledge going around on the north side to find a way up the summit outcrop. 5. Note in the register the names of a one- and a three-year-old child (the one-year-old was carried) that made the climb with their parents. Many people call this area a rugged wilderness. To some it's just their backyard.

Crow Mountain, foreground, from the north. Summit is on the south side of the sickle-shaped ridge. Bridge Point is just beyond.

Emigrant Peak overlooks the Yellowstone River valley. —Rick Reese

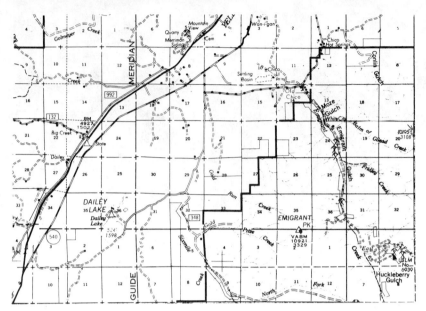

Boulder Mountain 10633 [S] Register. Northeast ramp completes the route from Speculator Creek.

The Needles 10905 [S] Register. From the south. The little spires on the north ridge are technical.

Arrow Peak 9122 [S] Southwest side.

The Pyramid 10730 [S] Register. West ridge straightforward, with other approaches just as interesting.

Crow Mountain 10721 [S] Register.

Bridge Point 10613 [S] One mile west of Elk Lake.

Chico Peak 10195 [S] Register. Attain the west ridge from Chico Hot Springs. Other variants on the west and south sides.

Point 10530 [S] West ridge. This point is on Chico Ridge, 1½ miles south of Chico Peak.

■ **Emigrant Peak 10921** [S] Turn east off Highway 89 at Emigrant, 23 miles south of Livingston, and cross the river. Then turn right on Highway 540 and travel a little over three miles. Now turn left onto a gravel road and head straight south, taking no turnoffs, for about three miles. Park. This is private land, so get permission to cross it if posted. Now inspect the west side of the mountain and climb it any way you want. You can vary your ascent and descent routes according to your taste. The north peak, 10558', is ½ mile from the higher south peak, where there is a register. The west ridge of the south peak is a popular route. The mountain itself is popular because it is dominant, accessible, easy, and has a great view. Still, it is a full day trip.

East end of the Mt. Wallace ridge

East side of Ash Mountain —U.S. Forest Service

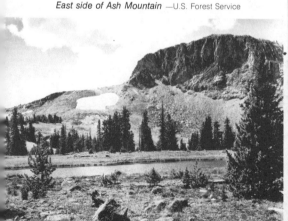

enes from Cowan's south ridge

Dome Mountain 8596 [S] A large abrupt hill, timbered on top. Take the southeast shoulder.

Mineral Mountain 10353 [S] Register. Southwest approach.

Monitor Peak 10420 [C] Register. Northwest side from trail. A little rock climbing on the summit knob.

Sheep Mountain 10587 [S] Southwest side from trail.

Ash Mountain 10243 [S] East side.

Mt. Wallace 10697 [S] Register. Southwest ridge. This peak is on a long ridge which trails off to the east and has many summits over 10000'.

Iron Mountain 10477 [S] Get on the south ridge from either side.

Hummingbird Peak 10015 [S] Southwest ridge.

   Technical Opportunities: The southern portion is fair-to-poor climbing on volcanic residuals. The northern portion is really swell. The most spectacular granite formations are concentrated in the Cowan cirque, with plenty of discoveries to the north and east (including The Needles spires) waiting for you. Just outside the Cowan cirque, west of Strawberry Mountain, is a lofty tusk, The Black Spire. It has a register and is best ascended up the east side from the head of Strawberry Creek (private access). Ice opportunities are scattered among the higher peaks, typified by two couloirs in Cowan's spires, and one on Black Mountain. The North Absaroka is rough, tough, and secretive.

199

Storm over Chrome Mountain

ake Mountain from Rainbow Lakes

Snowy Peak, summit cairn of Mt. Douglas in foreground

The Absaroka Range—East

"Mountains, ye are growing old;
your ribs of granite are getting weak and rotten."

—E. M. Morse

Description: A stark rock-strewn plateau. Elevation span 7700'. Higher peaks set back toward the central portion, with long approaches above timberline. Peaks to the south vegetated and less drastic.

Geology: Volcanoes were dominant. To the east, Precambrian basement rocks and granites of the adjacent Beartooth Plateau are common.

Access: South of Big Timber. Trails to the plateau start from the Boulder River Road (Highway 298) and the Stillwater River Road (Highway 419).

Ownership: Gallatin and Custer national forests.

Sliderock Mountain 7537 [S] Get on the Grouse Ridge Road to approach the timbered summit. Iron Mountain, 6932', on the north end of Grouse Ridge, has an open top for better views.

Sut Point 9319 [W] On Squaw Peak ridge. Alpine timber, short scramble from trail at 9191'.

Sugarloaf Mountain 7950 [S] West ridge from Lodgepole Creek trail. Timbered top.

Limestone Butte 7506 [W] Old lookout site.

Chrome Mountain 10150 [S] High point of the East Boulder Plateau.

Picket Pin Mountain 9995 [S] Short scramble from trail or road.

Iron Mountain 10088 [S] Short trip from encircling jeep road.

Snowy Peak 11075 [S] Highest summit of this broad mountain on the northeast ridge of Mt. Douglas.

Mt. Douglas 11298 [S] New register box installed 1980. Scrambling routes are unnecessary epics. They include bushwhacking four miles up Hawley Creek (Ugh!) then scrambling up the southwest side, bushwhacking two miles up Hawley Creek and coming up the northwest ridge

South side of Mt. Douglas from Point 11112

Beartooth Plateau from Mt. Douglas

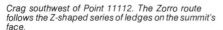

Crag southwest of Point 11112. The Zorro route follows the Z-shaped series of ledges on the summit's face.

East Boulder Plateau's flanks, nearly a mile high

after clawing up to a cirque splitting the trailing end of the ridge (Yuck!), or heading northwest from Upper Rainbow Lake to a meadow saddle and down the other side past a long lake in a narrow pass, dropping 500' (Urgh!). From there you'd angle right to the southwest side of Douglas, and the top.

Opt for one of two more direct C-rated routes with moderate exposure. Expect to spend time finding the route, and be careful. The northeast ridge from Snowy Peak is the more exposed route. If you're in doubt, bring a rope. The rock is crumbly.

The south ridge, or Doug-less route is more complicated, but the rock is better and the exposure more tolerable. First climb Point 11112 and cross the west end of its summit plateau to the rocky ridge heading north to Douglas. Descend this ridge to the saddle, using an exposed gully on the west side when the ridge gets steep. Continue on the ridge, climbing over two small outcrops, then head up the third much-larger outcrop until it gets vertical. Traverse onto the east side and scout out a route just below the sheer cliffs above you to traverse the east side of the ridge. It's not a straightforward route, but in time you should end up at a dihedral about 20' high. Climb halfway up it and take the ledge you find around to the edge of the rubble field, which you'll cross as you scramble the rest of the way to the summit. On your return, follow the ducks you set on the ascent.

Point 11112 (Mt. Doug-less) [S] The south peak of the Mt. Douglas group. Climbers on Lake Plateau have zipped up its south side or southeast ridge, thinking it was mighty Mt. Douglas, only to find that peak still off to the north, with intervening terrain of a discouraging nature. Hence its nickname.

■ **Lake Mountain 10800** [S] Take Highway 298 south out of Big Timber. Pass through McLeod and continue into the Boulder River Canyon. Automotive parts you don't want should be hanging loose so they can be torn off by boulders in the road. About five miles past the Fourmile Guard Station is Hicks Campground. Park at the upper end of it and walk up the road to the Upsidedown Creek Trailhead. You are now 47 miles south of Big Timber. It's seven miles of steep but well-designed trail to Rainbow Lakes, 3000' above. Now stroll to Upper Rainbow Lake (the third one), scramble through scattered timber on a slope east of the inlet, cross a rocky flat, and head up the broad south ridge of the mountain. To make the climb in a day, start early and wear shoes to run the trail with.

202   *Lake Plateau, where climbers cross rock meadows to their chosen peak*

In August 1938 the world was embroiled in uncertainty and headed for war. Yet this ranger and his horse found sun and snows of the mountains and streams flowing on regardless. You can still find that today in these meadows on the East Fork of the Boulder River. Sheepherder Peak's east ridge, center horizon —U.S. Forest Service

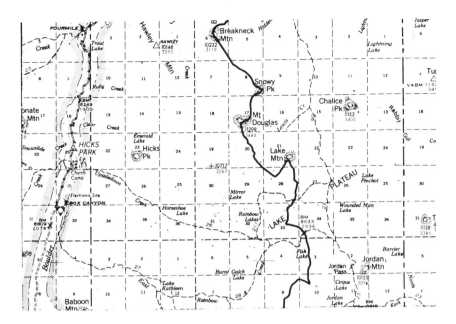

Chalice Peak 11153 [S] North or south ridge.

Tumble Mountain 11324 [S] Southeast ridge.

Two Sisters 11188 [C] Scramble up the west peak, 11138', then thread along the connecting ridge to the higher east peak. Steep snowfields clog this route until late summer.

Monument Peak 10995 [S] Register. Haystack Peak, just east, is also a scramble and has a register.

Sheepherder Peak 10800 [S] High point of this mountain is on its picturesque east ridge.

Pinnacle Mountain 10685 [S]

Mosquito Mountain 10417 [S] From the south.

Cutoff Mountain 10691 [S] Not the north side. A good example of volcanic sediments.

Mineral Mountain 10531 [S] From the south.

Miller Mountain 10484 [S] South side.

Sheep Mountain 10603 [S] Any approach except the east.

Technical Opportunities: You have volcanic palisades, somewhat firm aretes, and scattered boulders. You have big walls on many peaks. You have quality granite towers above the Stillwater River. You have unlimited opportunities. You also have a way to go, as the best formations are way up high. Cathedral Point, for instance, is a 2000' climb just to the base. The east side faces the Stillwater River and provides seven or eight pitches for a long day or possible overnighter. More good granite is in the far-removed north cirque of Two Sisters.

Two Sisters from the north. The summmit is left, behind the ridge cleaving the north cirque.

Wolf Glacier and Wolf Mountain

Western Ramparts, Beartooths. Stillwater River valley, foreground

The Beartooth Range

". . . How pleasing to come back this year
To Beartooth Wilderness, with comrade eyes
Recalling, as my own, familiar scenes
Of gracious granite spires in friendly skies
Where we may share again high enterprise."

—John Filsinger

Description: A massive south-sloping plateau. Gradual but visible 9500' elevation span. Loose rock fields and craggy peaks with very little vegetation.

Geology: The north end uplifted on a long fault. Everything younger than four billion years slid into Wyoming, exposing basement rock (formed just after the planet materialized). Glaciation and severe weathering did the finishing touches.

Access: West of Red Lodge. Trails and cross country routes are used on the plateaus. Jumping-off points for the West Rosebud Plateau are from Cooke City (Highway 212), Mystic Lake (gravel road from Fishtail on Highway 419), and East Rosebud Lake (from Roscoe on Highway 78). The Beartooth Plateau is usually reached from the West Fork Rock Creek Trailhead, west of Highway 212 at Red Lodge.

Ownership: Custer National Forest.

Background: Weather is a greater obstacle than the mountains. Winds of 100 miles per hour, lightning, and heavy snowfall can occur *any time*. A climbing team in 1939 reported, "The weather was fine on the ascent and we shed some of our clothing, but as we began the descent we found ourselves in one of those quickly born mountain storms that closed visibility to about four feet." Weather forecasts will help in planning your trip,

East side Mt. Hague

South side of Mt. Wood

Southwest side of Sawtooth Mountain. Wolf
Mountain northwest end of ridge —U.S. Forest Service

Mt. Zimmer from the southeast

but when scattered afternoon thunderstorms over the mountains are mentioned, be prepared. Since most summer storms develop in the afternoon, climb in the morning, finishing by two p.m.

Many climbing opportunities are made possible or enjoyable only by camping out. The East Rosebud area is heavily used, and campsites are limited, so consider a location closer to your chosen peak. Regardless of where you camp, stoves are useful as there is no firewood near the peaks.

On high plateaus watch for yellowish-brown wet spots of decomposed granite. These patches of "alpine quicksand" can bog you down, and have nearly swallowed horses.

Registers are not indicated in this chapter, as all the 12000' points except Granite Peak have them, and also Mt. Wilse, Wolf Mountain, and Beartooth Spire. As of last report the Forest Service is removing registers from wilderness peaks in the Beartooths when encountered. That's why there is no register on Granite Peak.

WEST OF EAST ROSEBUD CREEK

Twin Peaks 11800 [S]

Mt. Hague 12328 [S] South side from Island Lake. A popular C-rated route is the northeast cirque from Lake Wilderness.

Mt. Wood 12661 [S] Spend the first day bushwhacking up to the plateau from Mystic Lake. The second day you'll have the run of the place. It's little more than a grunt from the north, via Benbow Mine to Lake Wilderness, but then you'll have to cross an active rock slide—less desirable than the southern approach. Montana's second highest peak also has simple technical routes on its north side. A couloir on the north face, sometimes icy, is reached from a saddle on the northwest ridge. A chockstone blocks the couloir. Pitons have been effective on this short aid pitch. Another route is the northwest ridge, with rappels past gendarmes and notches.

Pyramid Mountain 12151 [S] South or northwest side.

Little Park Mountain 11506 [S]

Big Mountain 11371 [S]

Wolf Mountain 11850 [C] West ridge. Usually the couloir on the southwest side is full of snow. You'll need ice axes and a rope. A technical route, the vertical north face is on firm granite.

Sawtooth Mountain 11489 [T] Exposed rock from any direction. A steep snow chute on the north can be used to get close.

Iceberg Peak 11520 [S] From saddle north of the peak, reached from Goose Lake. Just east of the saddle is Grasshopper Glacier. A horde of locusts was deposited there by a storm a couple of centuries ago and covered by heavy snows. Warm weather had exposed some of the millions of imbedded specimens when the glacier was discovered about the turn of the century. The locusts are now harder to find, but still worth a look in late summer.

Mt. Zimmer 11550 [C] South side from Zimmer Creek, or from Goose Lake by climbing over a ridge. Near the top expect a little rock climbing, depending on snow in the gullies and your route choice. A technical route has been put up the northwest face.

Fox Peak 11245 [S]

Classic view of Granite's north face and east ridge, from the northwest flank of Tempest Mountain —U.S. Forest Service

Southeast side of Granite Peak, showing final 600' of the east ridge above the snowbridge

Mt. Wilse 11700 [S] Any side except the north.

Mystic Mountain 12063 [S] From the northeast.

Glacier Peak 12351 [S] South approach includes scrambling over big boulders. Also climbed from a saddle east of the peak, reached from Hidden Glacier. East ridge from the saddle C-rated. A prominent snow couloir ending under the summit on the northeast side is technical on both ice and rock. The couloir is exited left on exposed rock (about 5.4). On the north side of the peak, rock is exposed for 2000'.

Mt. Villard 12337 [S] South side, either via the west peak (12319') or the saddle between them. If you try the north ridge, rope up.

Granite Peak 12799 [T] Near the end of the last century, the U.S. Geological Survey was determining heights of major peaks and found this to be highest in Montana. Members of the survey made the first attempt to scale the peak in 1889 but were turned back by cliffs near the top. Three more tries were repulsed, including a 1914 attempt where storms and lack of firewood forced the expedition to burn its walking sticks. Finally in 1923 an assault was made on two routes by different teams, one successful. Between then and 1956 the top was reached by 26 climbers. Since them, attempts have increased to the present level of 1000 persons each year, with a couple of hundred making the top. Elevation and crowds aside, the peak is unique and interesting and offers a worthwhile confrontation.

Warnings about Beartooth weather go double for Granite Peak. The approach is long and usually involves crossing Froze-to-Death Plateau, home of lashing rain and cutting wind. On the peak rain or snow strike quickly, rendering the rock slick and hazardous. The route itself is neither simple or secure. Don't do Granite as your first mountain. Beforehand you need to acquire intermediate rock climbing skill, be able to find a route, and know how to belay a fellow climber on a

Glacier Peak (left) and Mt. Villard from the south

Granite Peak massif from the north, showing Storm Lakes. Behind are Cathedral Spires (barely visible, center), Mt. Villard, and Glacier Peak (right margin). —U.S. Forest Service

East side of Tempest Mountain, high point of Froze-to-Death Plateau. Note the many technical rock and snow routes. Granite Peak, center skyline

rope. You'll have to know how to deal with bad weather and altitude. The air is thin, 63% of sea-level pressure on the summit. You'll also have to be able to recognize the symptoms of hypothermia. Every year there are mishaps, and sometimes difficult rescue operations to this remote, rugged area are initiated. Occasionally rescues are not possible. One winter climb on the north side turned into an epic of survival as a team attempted to retreat from impossible conditions. It took several days to get off the mountain. One climber was badly frostbitten.

Granite Peak has only one route without major problems, the east ridge. It gets progressively more difficult as the summit is neared. The approach is usually made over Froze-to-Death Plateau or up Huckleberry Creek, though a longer, more fatiguing boulder hop from the southeast is possible.

Froze-to-Death Plateau can be reached from Mystic Lake, but the trail from East Rosebud Lake, longer but not so steep, is also suitable. The trail across the plateau, marked by cairns, swings north of Froze-to-Death Mountain. A one-night camp is necessary and can be placed at about 11700'. (Remember your minimum-impact camping.) The Huckleberry Creek approach requires staying out two nights at 10000', but camp is sheltered from weather ravaging the plateau. On summit day head for the col at the base of Granite's east ridge, between it and Tempest Mountain. If coming from the plateau, traverse the west side of Tempest to reach the col.

Scramble up the east ridge, noting possible bivouac sites should you need them on the descent. Half-way up is the famous snowbridge, actually a narrow ridge of snow at the top of two chutes dropping precipitously on both sides. This is the technical part of the climb. The snowbridge changes from year to year and during the climbing season. You'll need a rope for a safe belayed crossing. Bring one ice ax, as the bridge is sometimes knife-edged and may need to be widened for safety. Except for this spot the climb is rated C, so once across stash the rope if the weather looks good. Otherwise you may want it if you have to descend wet rock.

Step off to the left (south) side of the snowbridge, then look for a break so as to get back on the main ridge quickly. After a short stretch just over the north side of the ridge, the remainder of the route, sometimes intricate, follows the ridgetop or south side of it. Generally, it angles up through the top of an arête dropping to the south. Nearer the peak a steep gully with small chimneys must be climbed. The worst chimney can be bypassed on the right. Work around outcrops and hop along ledges. There are no really unsavory moves, but any deviation from the route leads to really difficult ones. Past climbers have set ducks to mark the route, and many ducks successfully overwinter. You simply need patience to find the route. Have plenty of time, and always, always watch the weather.

The summit can be reached by several technical routes. The south and southwest sides have short 5.4 or 5.5 climbs ending just west of the summit. The west ridge is a lofty traverse with several rappels. The north face has the most popular routes, and has been successfully ascended in winter. Summer or winter, you'll need ice ax and crampons along with your rock equipment. Once above the glacier (big bergschrund), there are several columns or arêtes to choose from. The central one, which tops out just west of the summit, has a triangular diamond of unfragmented rock at its base. Its left side is the easier line, about 5.4 to 5.6. Variants thereof, or the right side, get into 5.8 or 5.9.

Tempest Mountain 12478 [S] A good alternative if you have problems with Granite Peak.

Mt. Peal 12415 [S] Northeast or southeast approaches are interesting cross-country jaunts.

Froze-to-Death Mountain 11765 [S] Heap of rubble, easily reached from trail above Mystic Lake.

Beartooth Plateau, upper reaches of East Rosebud Creek down below —U.S. Forest Service

Castle Mountain. West peak, 12529', foreground, is climbed by the ramp visible on the southwest face.

EAST OF EAST ROSEBUD CREEK

Mt. Dewey 11436 [S] From either the north or south.

Sylvan Peak 11943 [S] East side from Lake Mary.

Elk Mountain 12192 [S] Gain saddle between Elk Mountain and Sylvan Peak from the east side.

Mt. Inabnit 11924 [S] The summit is a wedge-shaped knob.

Bowback Mountain 12343 [S] Climb Elk Mountain first, then walk the broad connecting ridge. East side approach also practical. South ridge has a deep cut in it, a technical crossing.

Sundance Mountain 12272 [S] From the east via Ship Lake. A large flat peak with two summits a mile apart. West summit 12206'.

Castle Rock Mountain 12408 [S] From Flat Rock Lake. Southwest ridge has goat trail to the top.

Castle Mountain 12612 [S] Gain saddle on the southeast ridge from either side. Follow ridge up.

■ **Silver Run Peak 12542** [S] Take the West Fork of Rock Creek Road at the south end of Red Lodge and follow it to the end, 14 miles. Dash up the trail to Sundance Pass, ten miles away and 3400' up. Maybe you'd enjoy the trip more if you camped along the way. Once at the pass, strike left (northeast) and ascend two miles of sloping rock meadows to the summit, the closer or westernmost of two peaks. The east peak is 12500'. Take it slow and allow plenty of time. Less than ⅔ of the oxygen at sea level is available here.

This climb is a spectacular, easy introduction to the really high country. To make a one-day climb, take the Timberline Lake Trail instead. Near the lake pick a break to the right (northwest) to

Whitetail Peak from the west. Mt. Lockhart and Sundance Pass left of it

West face of Silver Run Peak. Sundance Pass, right. Bowback Mountain's south ridge, lower portion of photo, with the deep cut near the left margin

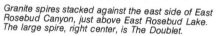
Granite spires stacked against the east side of East Rosebud Canyon, just above East Rosebud Lake. The large spire, right center, is The Doublet.

View from Sundance Pass, southwest up West Fork of Rock Creek. Saddle used to gain the southeast ridge of Castle Mountain on right skyline. Whitetail Peak, left. Note the great ice couloir on it reaching to the summit. —U.S. Forest Service

gain Silver Run Plateau.

From the summit look down the west face, which drops 3500' to the West Fork of Rock Creek. Technical climbs on this face take a couple of days, coming up the great arete called The Nose. It's about 5.8 or 5.9 on the right side of it, 5.11 up the middle. Silver Run Peak is a perfect example of most mountains in the Beartooths: The easy ways are really easy; the hard ways are really hard.

Mt. Lockhart 11647 [S] Summit ½ mile from 11000' Sundance Pass. Flat top.

Whitetail Peak 12548 [S] From Sundance Pass come up the northeast ridge right over Mt. Lockhart. The ice couloir on the north side runs 2000' (more early in the season) at a sustained 50 degrees. You need a rope. You need ice axes. And you need crampons.

Beartooth Mountain 12377 [C] Southeast shoulder or the south cirque, reached from Black Canyon Lake. All other sides of this massive block are vertical faces or ridges, some with glacial aprons around their bases. Routes of about 5.6 have been done up the north face (1500') and the northeast ridge, with a 5.9 performance on the northeast face.

Mt. Rearguard 12204 [S] Summit plateau reached by a series of large ledges from Sliderock Lake.

Point 12019 (Metcalf Mountain) [S] Unmapped, between Glacier and Moon lakes. Southeast ridge. Technical routes up the north side.

Lonesome Mountain 11409 [S] East side.

Grizzly Peak 9416 [J] Ski lift to top. Easy way to get a good view.

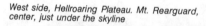
Beartooth Spire, summit of Beartooth Mountain behind

West side, Hellroaring Plateau. Mt. Rearguard, center, just under the skyline

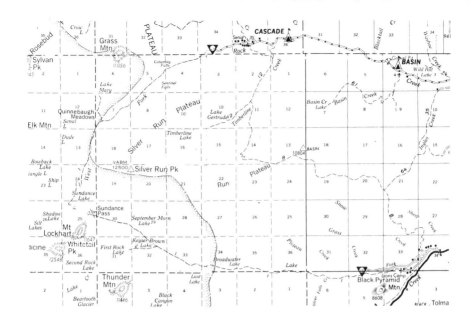

Technical Opportunities: Clean equipment, such as nuts and slings, are used for protection or aid. Bolts and pitons aren't necessary, as the rock is sufficiently cracked. In fact, it is unlikely you will find blank faces with hairline cracks. Here weather is definable by arctic standards, the rock is as old as rock can be, and altitude causes extreme daily temperature fluctuations. The resulting formations are heavily fractured, and all except the most appealing features tend to be disguised as debris. Also, a day is needed just to reach most formations. Many of the wall opportunities are all-day efforts, so you need to start draping rope at dawn.

Whatever austere project you choose, the countless other possibilities in the surrounding terrain are overwhelming. Only major canyons and obvious spires have been scouted out, and it will be many years before all the vertical dimensions are investigated.

West Rosebud Canyon: The granite is less fractured than elsewhere in the range. The two most popular crags are The Bulge and Power Tower, both south of the creek, near the Mystic Lake Hydroelectric Plant. The Bulge is four or five pitches. Power Tower, above it, is a half-day affair. Short (one or two pitch) climbs are found across the canyon.

East Rosebud Canyon: Just below East Rosebud Lake, west of the creek is a row of four formations with assorted climbs of two to seven pitches. First is the Tower of Incubus (nightmare). Then comes the Tower of Innocence, a pillar off the main cliff, a long day of 5.4 to 5.8, harder routes optional. Third is the Tower of Poor Rock. Last is The Ramp, seven pitches. Other crags are scattered among these larger ones, and little spires are high above the lake on the west side.

Up the canyon on the east side of the lake is a dramatic series of formations, beginning with Camels Hump and Chocolate Drop. Up near Snow Creek is The Doublet, a large tower of good rock high above the valley. The first pitches are vertical, then the face leans back. This is 5.7 to 5.9, with aid, two days needed, bivy cave half-way. Adjacent towers, some unexplored, would take two or more days. Should you be tempted to try the large rounded structure between Elk and Rimrock lakes, be advised that the north face is a bad piece of rock with rotten overhangs. Its west buttress is a wiser choice.

 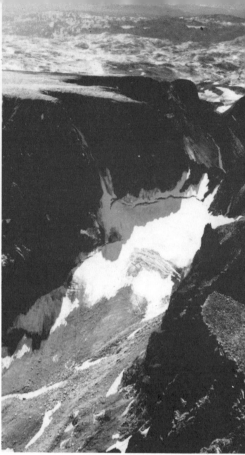

Little spire on the northwest ridge of Mt. Wood. Features great and small make up the Beartooth landscape.

There are 186 different rock and ice routes hidden near Snowbank Mountain. How many can you find? How many can you climb?

West Fork of Rock Creek: Scattered crags are past the end of the road, including associated outcrops of the west face route on Silver Run Peak.

High walls: Nearly every peak in the beartooths, including unlisted lower summits, has exciting walls and aretes. For instance, there's a six pitch climb through ledge systems of the "X" formation on the east face of Mt. Shepard.

High Spires: Several points in the range can be reached only by diligent application of protection. The west ridge of Granite Peak has one such pinnacle, a small arete. South of there, on the southeast ridge of Mt. Villard are the 12000' elevation Cathedral Spires, an impressive array of shining towers. The Shark Fin, on the northeast flank of Castle Mountain's west peak, at 12500' is the state's highest free-standing spire. Its base can be reached by a glacier climb, or by a rappel off the west peak. Beartooth Spire, 11915', the namesake of the range, resembles a bear's tooth. The east side is 5.6, maybe 5.7. The west side, from the notch between it and Beartooth Mountain, is about 5.9. There are other routes.

Snow and Ice Climbs: Just above Glacier Lake, on the Wyoming state line, are ice climbs. June Couloir, a popular snow gully, can be seen from the highway to the east. In winter, water ice is often available at Break-A-Leg Falls in the Snow Creek area of the East Rosebud, and on both sides of the highway near Cooke City. There are, of course, many glaciers high on the Beartooth Plateau, and at the head of West Rosebud Creek.

Escarpments of the Pryors

The Lower Yellowstone Area

"My love is the valley, the breezes that sigh
My love is the mountains that reach to the sky
My love is the·valley, the rocks and the rills
My love is the prairie, the low rolling hills
The low rolling hills."

—Marty Robbins

Description: Grassy rises and buttes. Larger hills, usually timbered, from Hardin east to the state line. The Pryors, real mountains, are two broad grassy ramps. The north end of the Bighorns, at the Wyoming state line, rises 5600' above Bighorn Reservoir. Otherwise, prominent features are miniature, such as badland peaks and ridges.

Geology: Fort Union Formation, strata deposited during an era of prolific plant life, when coal seams formed under much of the area. An ancient sea accounts for sandstone at Chalk Buttes and Medicine Rocks. The Bull Mountains are uplands of more erosion-resistant sandstone interspersed with coal. Sandstone layers in the Wolf Mountains are inclined. Badlands around Glendive, Miles City, and Fort Peck Reservoir are deposits of the Hell Creek Formation from the dinosaur age. The Pryors are an uplifted dome of Madison limestone, 300 million years old. From East Pryor Mountain, the same limestone appears thousands of feet below in Bighorn Canyon.

The Sand Arroyo Badlands

Northeast side of Big Pryor Mountain drops sharply.
Technical equipment for climbing the Pryors

Access: East of Billings, south of the Missouri River. County roads and highways from Interstates 90 and 94 reach into all areas. Individual locales are usually served by truck roads.

Ownership: Custer National Forest, Crow and Northern Cheyenne Indian reservations, Lewistown and Miles City districts Bureau of Land Management, and private.

THE FORT PECK RESERVOIR AREA

No prominent points in this area. Low hills and buttes provide views. The reservoir (2246') is large, and there are places where you can't see the other side. A boat will get you to York Island (2321') for views of the rugged breaks. On the upland to the south are the Hell Creek Badlands, east of which are points such as Brownie Butte (2762', in Section 15, Township 22 North, Range 40 East) and Signal Butte (2765', two miles south of Brownie Butte). Highest elevation west of Hell Creek is 3384', west of Brusett. On the east side of the reservoir, elevations approach 2500' near the Dry Creek inlet. North of Rock Creek and west of Highway 24 are the Sand Arroyo Badlands, with up to 500' of relief. Eternity speaks with a loud voice here. Sagebrush and windswept pastel-colored formations are the ghost towns of dinosaurs and ancient seaside jungles.

THE SIDNEY BUTTES AREA

Small hills dot the plains west of Sidney. They include Big Enough Point (2552', in the Tree Buttes ten miles south of Culbertson, two miles east of the highway), Lone Butte (2600', just west of Sidney), and Blue Hill (2645', 20 miles northwest of Sidney, with radio facilities).

THE BULL MOUNTAINS

Dunn Mountain 4744 [S] Southwest approach from Holland Mine, five miles east of Highway 87. The Fattig Creek Road goes to the eastern reaches of the plateau. Head west four miles to an overlook. The south rim of this mountain is called Red Bluff.

Three Buttes 4627 [S] From the south or east. South of Musselshell.

THE EAST MUSSELSHELL—BIG SHEEP AREA

An area of prairie separating the Missouri and Yellowstone river basins. High points are small buttes and low-profile grassy domes, several around 3600'. Maximum elevation, 3723', just west of Sumatra. Big Sheep Mountain, 3625', south of Circle, is a prairie uplift.

Meadows, west slope of East Pryor Mountain
Buttes near the Powder River have light colored strata and patchy timber. —Bill Cunningham

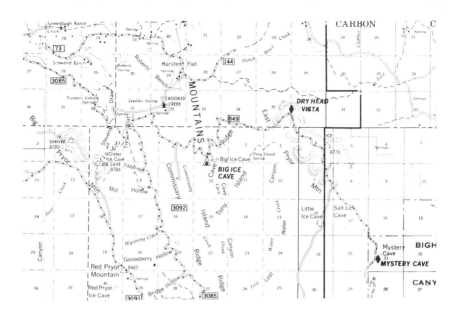

THE PINE HILLS AREA

Buttes and badlands around Miles City and Glendive. Both the Makoshika and Terry badlands top out about 2700'. Just west of Terry is a scenic view, 2780', reached by a P-rated road. Another overlook is Signal Butte, 3092', three miles east of Miles City. It can be reached by trail. During the Indian Wars the army sent mirror signals from here to far-flung troops. To the east and away from the Yellowstone River are scattered islands of buttes in a sea of ranchland. Many surpass 3000'. High points include 3372' south of Wibaux, 3373' east of Miles City, 3422' west of Baker, and 3551' two miles southeast of Willard.

THE PRYOR MOUNTAINS

Black Butte 5148 [J] Bow Point on some maps. Thirteen miles southeast of Bridger.
West Pryor Mountain 6688 [W] Short hike from jeep road.
Big Pryor Mountain 8786 [D] A car might not make this trip when the road is wet.
Red Pryor Mountain 8465 [D] Grassy top.
■ **East Pryor Mountain 8776** [W] A Custer National Forest map will help on the roads around Pryor. Head south out of Pryor for about 16 miles, through Pryor Gap, then turn left and go up Sage Creek. Follow signs 23 miles past the Big Ice Cave to Dry Head Vista. From there the road gets rough, but when dry a car can make it. You'll come out of the trees 1½ miles past the vista. Park, step through a fence, and stroll to the top, where you'll find a wooden triangulation tower. Walk to the northeast for views of the prairie and Bighorn Canyon a mile below.

THE BIGHORN MOUNTAINS

Windy Point 9132 [D] Lookout building. One mile south, the state line crosses the crest of the range at 9257'. A 42-mile drive southwest out of Lodgegrass.

THE WOLF MOUNTAINS

Several small ranges between the Little Bighorn and Tongue rivers. Buttes numerous north of Lame Deer and around Colstrip. Rosebud Buttes (3380' for the middle one) are just off Rosebud Creek Road eight miles south of Rosebud. Near Lame Deer, the Little Wolf Mountains (4820') to the northwest are semi-timbered and served by jeep trails.

Rosebud Point 5217 [P] Lookout tower. The road heads east from Lodge Grass.
Red Point 5450 [S] A P-rated road approaches from the south to within a mile.
Busby Butte 4543 [S] West side, or east side using a jeep trail.
Crazy Horse Point 4792 [W] Eleven miles southeast of Busby. Short walk from a P-rated road.
Bull Creek Point 4707 [P] Lookout site.

215

Sandstone towers poke out of the prairie in the Medicine Rocks. —U.S. Forest Service

Badger Peak 4422 [D] A grassy dome with a lookout tower named Morningstar Lookout. Turn north off Highway 212 five miles east of Lame Deer. Drive one mile.

Garfield Peak 4316 [S] Twelve miles northeast of Lame Deer. Drive within a mile on a truck road, then take the west ridge.

Point 4401 [P] Seven miles east of Lame Deer, just south of Highway 212.

Fisher Butte 4396 [P] Twelve miles south of Lame Deer.

Cook Creek Butte 4505 [P]

THE ASHLAND AREA

The eastern side, along the Powder River, has numerous buttes 200' high. Several points, 4000', are on the east side of the Tongue River near Birney. The road just west of Quietus climbs to 4200'.

Liscom Butte 4341 [P] Maintained lookout.

Home Creek Butte 4410 [P] Radio facilities. Seventeen miles east of Ashland.

King Mountain 4167 [S] South of Ashland.

Yager Butte 4124 [D] Maintained lookout tower. Road impassable to cars when wet.

Poker Jim Butte 4348 [D] Manned lookout. Picnic area and Tongue River view on top.

Gardner Butte 4300 [S] Seven miles south of Sonnette.

Diamond Butte 4301 [D] Manned lookout. The last mile may be too rough for your car.

THE BROADUS AREA

Buttes of 4000' or more are common within 30 miles of Broadus. North of there and 15 miles northwest of Powderville is Maxwell Butte, 3726'. South of Hammond, higher ground over 4000' includes Stack Rocks (4050') in Sections 21 and 22 of Township 9 South, Range 55 East. These rocks are scrambles or harder. To the east, Finger Buttes (4201') are also challenging little climbs. You may find the rock too flimsy to provide confidence with technical protection. Finger Buttes are 15 miles north of Albion. A truck can drive within two miles.

Bear Skull Mountain 4300 [S] Also mapped as Patten Point. Five miles northwest of Biddle.

Hammond Point 4193 [W] Two miles south of Hammond.

West Butte 4450 [J] Three miles north of Ridge.

THE EKALAKA AREA

Two unique sandstone features: One is Medicine Rocks along Highway 7, an assortment of small features to clamber on. The other is Capitol Rock, 3884', in the Long Pines. This easily eroded landmark has been damaged by people climbing on it. You can help preserve it by climbing anything else.

Big Hill 3948 [W] Southwest of Ekalaka.

Chalk Buttes 4215 [S] Access to these isolated plateaus provided from the east by the Trenk Pass Road, across private land. The buttes are flat-topped, timbered, and five miles from end to end.

Tri Point 4125 [D] Lookout tower standing above pine trees on a plateau.

Belltower Butte 4015 [S] East side from a truck road.

Sheep Mountain 4065 [S] From the west.

Technical Opportunities: The Rimrocks, a 200'-high sandstone wall dominating the north side of Billings and continuing east and west along the Yellowstone River, is truly a "backyard" climbing area. Rock quality is good enough to accept nuts, chocks, friends, etc., in cracks, but isn't well suited for face climbing or bolts and pitons. Top-roping is nearly always possible and should have been done by those who have had accidents. Popular routes are near Indian Cave east of town, below the KTVM television tower, above Eastern Montana College, and near Zimmerman Trail on the west edge of town. With all these spots readily available, you shouldn't need Pompeys Pillar, a 200' sandstone lump and historic landmark 25 miles east of Billings. Farther out are limited opportunities on limestone terraces along the Tongue River, and on Stag Rock (3460') near the Fort Howes Ranger Station. This 100' outcrop has been climbed, but its use is probably best limited to walking up the west side and rappelling off the top.

Climbing the Rimrocks. Expansion protection installed in a crack is fairly reliable.
—Marvin McDonald

Horizons

MONTANA,
Mighty Land . . .

"See the light ram through the gaps in the land." —Kate Bush

A mighty ship of the sky sails through an endless sea of cloud, on a million-year voyage.

*The mountains were here before we came,
and they will be here when we are gone.*

The urge to climb a mountain occurs when you see it for the first time, and it startles you.

"Climbing out, just hold your heading true.
Got to get your finest out.
You're number 1, anticipating you."

—Mike Oldfield

The quality of life improves when something has your undivided attention.

*"On the summit all is light, though the
full realization of the vast range of view
is subtly delayed . . . such sights
do not make their full impact at first."*

—Geoffrey Crankshaw

"On every mountain height is rest."

—Goethe

"As the clouds rose out of the valley a strong west wind levelled them off even with our summit, over which the wind was whipping rather violently. Each of us saw his shadow cast upon this sea of clouds, and around each shadow was a complete circle rainbow."

—J. Gordon Edwards on Heavens Peak

"And this voice which came from heaven we heard, when we were with him in the holy mount."

—2 Peter 1:18

*"I have climbed the hills and walked in remote places.
How could I have seen you save from a great height or a great
distance."*

—Kahlil Gibran

*. . . seeing the lights of a city where everybody
is warm and comfortable
and generally unappreciative of that,
while you are high and alone
in the dark with the cold wind at your back. . . .*

—Cal Tassinari

—U.S. Forest Service

"As the sun went down the light left the upper snowfields, the cliffs became faint and shadowy, the Turquoise Lake turned a deep sapphire. A slight breeze rippled the otherwise calm expanse and in places bright golden flecks of light shimmered on the surface. We reached camp dead tired at 7:15. It had been a very sporty climb, taken in the most difficult way possible in spite of our planning."

—"Mountaineering in the Mission Range in Montana" by Arthur C. Tate *Appalachian Mountain Club Bulletin* December, 1929.

—Kalispell Weekly News

*"We have not ceased from exploration
and the end of all our exploring
will be to arrive where we started
and know the place for the first time."*

—T. S. Eliot

the timeless wildness prevails. . . .

—Kalispell Weekly News

Glossary

arête — a steep outcrop or spur, with at least one vertical face or sharp ridge, attached to a larger formation, and sometimes separating cirques

batholith — lava that rose and cooled below the earth's surface to form a large dome of igneous rock

belay — the winding of a rope around an object to secure another object. In climbing, it is the use of friction on a rope to protect a climber.

bergschrund — the large crevasse where a glacier pulls away from a snowfield above it

bushwhack — to travel through heavy brush, timber, or downfall without benefit of a trail

cairn — a pile of rocks fitted together to mark a trail or summit

carabiner — an oval ring of hardened aluminum which has a hinged gate so it can be clipped into protection devices

chute — a gully or ditch on a steep slope which is often swept by rockfall or avalanches

cirque — a deep, steep-walled mountain basin shaped like half a bowl

clean — the ascent of a technical route using protection which is not permanently placed, and which will not normally alter the rock when removed

col — an exposed saddle, usually just below a peak

couloir — a steep gully high on a mountain, devoid of vegetation and sometimes containing snow and ice

crag — any steep rugged cliff or outcrop of rock

crampon — a steel frame with sharp points, used for climbing ice and snow, which fits onto a boot

crevasse — a split or cleavage in a glacier or snowfield

dihedral — a vertical rock column or face that abuts against a cliff at an angle

direct aid — the use of climbing hardware to install a handhold, foothold, or rest support

duck — a small stack of stones used to mark a climbing route

etrier — a piece of nylon webbing fashioned into a series of loops and used as a portable ladder in direct aid climbing

exposure — the sensation of danger or space experienced on a steep slope or cliff

flank — the side of a spur

free — the ascent of a technical route without the use of direct aid, but with the employment of protection

friction — a rock climbing technique where the foot is flattened or "smeared" onto the rock rather than edged on ledges or jammed into cracks

gendarme — a steep rock outcrop on a ridgetop

ice ax — a tool used on snow and ice slopes for balance, self-arrest, and chopping steps. It has a long handle with a spike on one end, and a head consisting of a long pick and an adze.

moat — a broad, deep crack separating a glacier or snowfield from adjacent rock

open book — a dihedral

pitch — the distance climbed between alternating belays on a technical route. It is usually slightly less than the length of the rope being used.

Precambrian — the first geologic period, taking in all time before the beginning of life

protection — the use of ropes and other climbing hardware on a technical ascent to save a climber in the event of a fall

rappel — to descend on a free hanging rope

register — a container on a summit holding the names and comments of climbers who have visited there

saddle — a low point on a ridge, or a low point between two peaks.

scree — a uniform type of talus composed of small rocks which slide easily. It can cover a slope up to the ridgetop or summit.

self-arrest — the use of an ice ax to stop a slide down a glacier or snowfield

shoulder — a very rounded ridge or spur

spur — a subsidiary ridge extending sideways from a major ridge

swale — a low area between two higher areas, usually grassy hummocks

talus — rock debris piled up at the foot of a mountainside or cliff

technical — a climb which uses climbing hardware to prevent or protect from a slip or fall

three point contact — a rock climbing principle where three of the four limbs are always held in contact with the route to provide control

traverse — to travel or climb across a slope rather than ascend it

variant — a detour or alternate line on a route

Roger Marshall

About the Author

Since 1969 Pat Caffrey has been on over 100 of Montana's prominent summits. He has also climbed throughout the Rockies and Cascades, on Baffin Island, and in the Yukon, Alaska, Japan, Australia, Peru, Argentina, and Antarctica.

After finishing high school in Glasgow, Montana, he earned a forestry degree from the University of Montana, and now lives in Seeley Lake where he works for a private timber company. He is a member of the Missoula County Sheriff's Search & Rescue. He built his own house and lives with his wife Debra and three children.